...TLAS OF

FIRST PEOPLES

A Future for the Indigenous World

Julian Burger

with campaigning groups
and native peoples worldwide

Foreword by Maurice F. Strong

A GAIA ORIGINAL

ANCHOR BOOKS
Doubleday
New York London Toronto Sydney Auckland

A GAIA ORIGINAL

Written by Julian Burger

Based on an idea by
Rosanne Hooper and Joss Pearson

Editorial
Rosanne Hooper
Joanna Godfrey Wood
Eleanor Lines

Design
Sara Mathews
Bridget Morley

Picture research
Susan Mennell

Illustration
Ann Savage

Production
Susan Walby

Copy preparation
Lesley Gilbert

An Anchor Book
Published by Doubleday
A division of Bantam Doubleday Dell Publishing Group, Inc.,
666 Fifth Avenue, New York, New York 10103

Anchor Books Doubleday and the portrayal of an anchor are trademarks of Doubleday, a division of Bantam Doubleday Dell Publishing Group, Inc.

FIRST ANCHOR BOOKS EDITION: October 1990
RRC

Library of Congress Cataloging-in-Publication Data applied for.

ISBN 0-385-26653-7

10 9 8 7 6 5 4 3 2 1

First US Edition

Filmset by Marlin Graphics Ltd, Sidcup, Kent
Reproduction by Technographic Design and Print Ltd, Suffolk
Printed and bound in Spain by Artes Graphicas Toledo, S.A.
DL TO: 278-1990

Consultants
The author expresses his warmest gratitude to the following readers for their enthusiasm and support for the project and their valuable comments which greatly enriched the text:

Joji Carino, Cordillera People's Alliance, the Philippines
Jason Clay, Cultural Survival, USA
Marcus Colchester, anthropologist, UK
Andrew Gray, International Work Group for Indigenous Affairs, Denmark
Jim Inaya, National Indian Youth Council, USA
Jacques de Kort, Workgroup for Indigenous Peoples, Netherlands
Roger Moody, Colonialism and Indigenous Research and Action, UK
Norman Myers, environmentalist, UK
Geoff Nettleton, anthropologist, UK
Jorje Tereno, Union of Indian Nations, Brazil
Sharon Venne, Treaty Six Area, Canada

Contributors
Many individuals and organizations, reflecting a wide range of views and experiences, also contributed with advice, research, comment and writing. The author especially thanks the following:
Pat Adams, Energy Probe, Canada
Gudmundur Alfredsson, United Nations Centre for Human Rights
Teresa Aparicio, Co-Director International Work

Group for Indigenous Affairs
Daniel Ashini, Innu people
Bob Barnes, Institute of Social Anthropology, University of Oxford
Russel Barsch, Four Directions Council
Howard Berman, California Western School of Law
Pierrette Birraux, Department of Geography, University of Geneva
Ivar Bjorklund, University of Tromso
Tica Broch, Minority Rights Group, UK
Carmel Budiardjo, TAPOL – The Indonesian Human Rights Campaign
Centre for Science and Environment, India
Mac Chiapin, Cultural Survival
Jason Clay, Cultural Survival
Paul Coe, Chairman National Aboriginal and Islander Legal Services
Fay Cohen, Dalhousie University, Nova Scotia
Marcus Colchester, anthropologist
Cultural Survival, Boston
Jens Dahl, Co-director International Work Group for Indigenous Affairs
Ken Deer, Haudonasaunee Nation
Documentation Centre for Indigenous Peoples, Geneva
Nancy Doubleday, Inuit Circumpolar Conference
Nicky Ebenau, Goldhawk Productions, London
Bob Epstein, adviser Grand Council of Cree
Pat Fowell, National Coalition of Aboriginal Organizations
Rene Fuerst, Chairman International Work Group for Indigenous Affairs
Gale Gomez, anthropologist
Andrew Gray, International Work Group for Indigenous Affairs
Govert de Groot, Workgroup for Indigenous Peoples
Hinewhare Harawira, Waitangi Action Committee
Olivia Harriss, Goldsmiths College, University of London
Margaret Herps, solicitor National Aboriginal and Islander Legal Services
Martin von Hildebrand, Amazon Rainforest Research Centre, Colombia
Luke Holland
Ngapare Hopa, Center for Maori Studies, University of Waikato
Maurice Howard, translator
Incomindios, Basel
Independent Commission on International Humanitarian Issues, Geneva
International Work Group on Indigenous Affairs, Copenhagen

M.I. Isaev, Institute of Linguistics, University of Moscow
John Kelly, Hawaii Nation
Jacques de Kort, Director Workgroup for Indigenous Peoples
Etto Krijger, Workgroup for Indigenous Peoples
Saskia Stenfert Kroese, Workgroup for Indigenous Peoples
Sharad Kulkarni, Centre for Tribal Conscientization, Pune
Atencio Lopez, Movimiento de la Juventud Kuna, Panama
Sarah Lundskar, University of Oslo
Carolyn Marr, TAPOL
Tracy Maree Maurer, journalist
Nganeko Kaihau Minhinnick, Maori People
V.C. Mohan, Sahabat Alam Malaysia
Brian Morris, Goldsmiths College, University of London
Ted Moses, Grand Council of the Cree
Mrinalini Murmu, India
Garth Nettheim, University of New South Wales
Geoff Nettleton, anthropologist
Stephen Nugent, Goldsmiths College, University of London
Moringe Parkipuny MP, Masai People
Darrell Posey, Museu Paraense Emilio Goeldi, Brazil
Ulises Rosas Campos, Indigenous World
Sahabat Alam Malaysia (Friends of the Earth)
Dalee Sambo, Inuit Circumpolar Conference
Isabelle Schulte-Tenckhoff, anthropologist
Mary Simon, President Inuit Circumpolar Conference
Katariana Sjoeberg, University of Lund, Sweden
Lars Softestad, Agder College, Norway
V.M. Solntsev, Director Institute of Linguistics, Academy of Sciences, USSR
Anapaula Sotomayor, Conselho Missionario Indigenista, Brazil
Kaye Stearman, Minority Rights Group
Line Stephenson, University of Copenhagen
Survival International, London
Lee Swepston, International Labour Office
Jeremy Swift, Institute of Development Studies, University of Sussex
Mililani Trask, Hawaii Nation
United Nations Centre on Transnational Corporations
Sharon Venne, Cree People, Treaty Six Area
Brigit Vonasch, Incomindios, Switzerland
Espen Waehle, NORAD, Norway
Ingrid Washinawatok, Indigenous Women's Network
Workgroup for Indigenous Peoples, Amsterdam

FOREWORD by Maurice F. Strong

Our Earth is a vulnerable, abused place. Its opulent forests are rapaciously felled, its rivers and oceans polluted, its already degraded soils worked lifeless, its delicate envelope of atmosphere – the very basis for life on this planet – is contaminated. In bending nature to our implacable will, we are also destroying her. Our material progress is achieved at the cost of passing on a wasteland to our grandchildren. As this turbulent century closes, we must alter radically our ways of life, patterns of consumption, systems of values, even the manner in which we organize our societies, if we are to ensure survival of the Earth, and ourselves.

As we reawaken our consciousness that humankind and the rest of nature are inseparably linked, we will need to look to the world's more than 250 million indigenous peoples. They are the guardians of the extensive and fragile ecosystems that are vital to the wellbeing of the planet. Indigenous peoples have evolved over many centuries a judicious balance between their needs and those of nature. The notion of sustainability, now recognized as the framework for our future development, is an integral part of most indigenous cultures.

In the last decades, indigenous peoples have suffered from the consequences of some of the most destructive aspects of our development. They have been separated from their traditional lands, and ways of life, deprived of their means of livelihood, and forced to fit into societies in which they feel like aliens. They have protested and resisted. Their call is for control over their own lives, the space to live and the freedom to live in their own ways. And it is a call not merely to save their own territories, but the Earth itself.

While no-one would suggest that the remainder of the more than 5 billion people on our planet would live at the level of indigenous societies, it is equally clear that we cannot pursue our present course of development. Nor can we rely on technology to provide an easy answer. What modern civilization has gained in knowledge, it has perhaps lost in sagacity. The indigenous peoples of the world retain our collective evolutionary experience and insights which have slipped our grasp. Yet these hold critical lessons for our future. Indigenous peoples are thus indispensible partners as we try to make a successful transition to a more secure and sustainable future on our precious planet.

CONTENTS

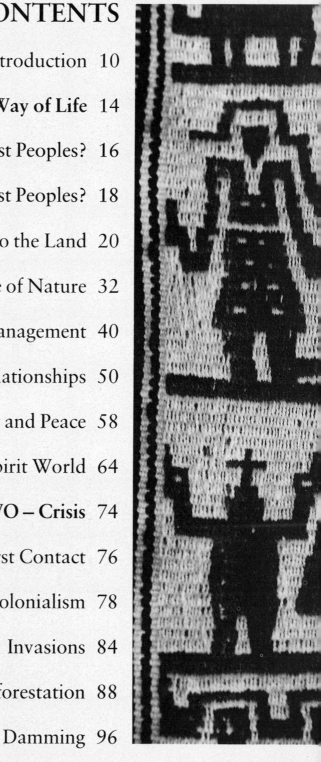

Author's note

This book is written in the belief that individuals can contribute to greater justice for indigenous peoples. Part, although not all, of the blame for the destruction of indigenous communities can be laid at the door of the rich. Governments, banks, and companies have often pursued policies and backed regimes that are unfavourable to indigenous peoples, mainly to supply market demand. It is the consumer's hands on the chain saw. But ordinary people are not powerless. We may each have a small voice, but when harmonized with others, we can make powerful institutions listen. If you wish to do something and to know more, the organizations listed at the back of the book would welcome your support.

The Gaia Atlas of First Peoples is the product of a collaboration of many different individuals and groups – indigenous contributors, human rights experts, concerned anthropologists, journalists. An overriding objective has been to reflect faithfully the concerns of first peoples – perhaps an impossible task given the range of their different experiences. At all stages – planning, writing and editing – native peoples have been closely involved. The book endeavours to bring together the multitude of views and situations of indigenous peoples, as shared with the author over a number of years in forest villages, outback communities, city slums, United Nations meetings, and many other places. It is the work of many, but the responsibility of its author/editor. If there are mistakes or misunderstandings they are his alone.

Julian Burger

INTRODUCTION

1992 marks a year not of celebration but of mourning for the first peoples of the Americas. In the 500 years since Christopher Columbus arrived, tragedy has taken its toll on the descendants of the continent's original inhabitants. Their numbers have been decimated. And today, indigenous peoples are the most disadvantaged groups in society, suffering the worst health, receiving the least education and among the very poorest. Peoples who retained some of their former territory have seen their lands taken over, and often destroyed, as outsiders fell forests and bring in roads, dams, mines, and plantations.

1992 is a year for indigenous peoples all over the world to reflect not only on the past but on strategies for dealing with today's abuses. For the 1990s are a time when indigenous communities are demanding that their lands be restored to them, that their cultures be protected and that their right to self-determination be recognized. Already the local, national and regional indigenous organizations that proliferated in the 1980s are becoming increasingly effective in their relationships with governments. And in some countries indigenous peoples are the single most persistent force for change. At the international level, they are actively campaigning for a Declaration of Indigenous Rights for proclamation by the United Nations General Assembly. As the world is poised to enter the new millennium, the indigenous world is demanding its own liberation.

The 1990s are also a time for indigenous peoples to reflect on their role in a changing global future. As environmental issues become increasingly urgent, and Western models of development and industrialization becomes daily less sustainable, indigenous peoples may

"We understand that many of these racialist attitudes are subconscious and not premeditated, but nevertheless they reflect how deeply dominant ideology has penetrated society." Mapuche Indian

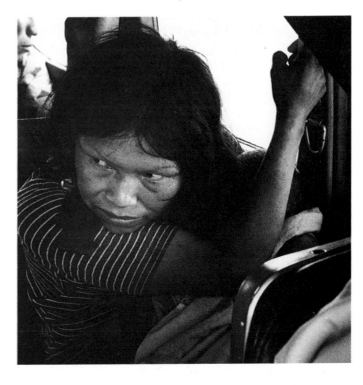

come to occupy a position of considerable influence. Their views on a possible union of development and conservation could become central to decision-making.

The Gaia Atlas of First Peoples is a book about the world's 250 million or more indigenous peoples. Part One describes their ways of life, their great diversity as well as the common values and experiences that they share. Part

"We're standing up and taking up the battle here and now to protect our young so their unborn can know the freedom our grandparents knew." Regina Brave, North American Indian

Two shows that indigenous peoples also share grave problems. Governments, banks, companies and advisers – whether Western or from the countries concerned – are all too often to blame. However well-meaning their aims, they have promoted political changes and economic development in the last thirty years that have profoundly disrupted indigenous communities worldwide. But, as Part Three demonstrates, indigenous peoples are

increasingly exposing abuses and misconceived schemes, and setting up their own more appropriate development programmes. A new international movement of indigenous peoples is promoting values that are increasingly recognized as of universal importance.

There are compelling reasons for being concerned about indigenous peoples. They are suffering silently a physical destruction virtually unknown to the rest of the world. Their situation on humanitarian grounds alone demands that the international community take action, for the loss of a unique culture diminishes the entire human family. There are strong legal grounds too. Indigenous peoples have not benefited from the process of decolonization. Yet the right to self-determination of peoples is legally enshrined in the Bill of Human Rights. Indigenous peoples are aware that they must realize their liberation in societies where they are in many cases a numerical minority. Few want political independence. But the majority want a sufficient economic base, and the right to manage their own affairs.

There are also self-interested reasons for supporting the struggle of indigenous peoples. As the wider society learns from those who have arrived at a long-term balanced relationship with the land, and contrasts this with modern, damaging technologies, we are beginning to acknowledge the failings of Western lifestyles and attitudes. The destruction of the great forests, tundra, savannas, and oceans, which we once thought could absorb our pollution indefinitely, is intimately related to all our futures. These are the last of the world's wild places and the needs of our increasing populations are pressing heavily upon them. Our best hope in saving these environments lies in a partnership with their traditional inhabitants. Instead of condemning indigenous peoples as an obstacle, we now have to see expansion itself as unsustainable.

The Gaia Atlas of First Peoples sets out to help us understand a little better the extraordinary human diversity of the world and to reflect on our way of managing affairs. We are often too arrogant to believe that other people might orga-

"At first I thought I was fighting to save rubber trees, then I thought I was fighting to save the Amazon rain forest. Now I realize I am fighting for humanity." Chico Mendez

nize their societies more successfully or have something to teach us – even about that most treasured of Western principles: freedom. Orlando Villas-Boas, who with his brothers, has spent half a century defending indigenous peoples in Brazil, observes: "If an individual shouts out in the centre of Sao Paulo, a police car may carry him off under arrest. If an Indian lets out an enormous yell in the middle of his village, no one will look at him, no one will ask him why he shouted. The Indian is a free man." And it is the freedom of indigenous peoples that is being fought for today.

PART ONE

WAY OF LIFE

Indigenous peoples are strikingly diverse in their culture, religion, and social and economic organization. Yet, today as in the past they are prey to stereotyping by the outside world. By some they are idealized as the embodiment of spiritual values; by others they are denigrated as an obstacle impeding economic progress. But they are neither: they are people who cherish their own distinct cultures, are the victims of past and present-day colonialism, and are determined to survive. Some live according to their traditions, some receive welfare, others work in factories, offices or the professions. As well as their diversity, there are some shared values and experiences among indigenous cultures. Where they have maintained a close living relationship to the land, there exists a co-operative attitude of give and take, a respect for the Earth and the life it supports, and a perception that humanity is but one of many species. This part of the book describes some aspects of the ways of life of indigenous peoples, particularly where they contrast with mainstream culture. By understanding how they organize their societies, the wider society may learn to recognize that they are not at some primitive stage of development, but thoughtful and skillful partners of the natural world, who can help all people to reflect on the way humanity treats the environment and our fellow creatures.

WHO ARE FIRST PEOPLES?

". . . it is an important and special thing to be an Indian. Being an Indian means being able to understand and live with this world in a very special way. It means living with the land, with the animals, with the birds and fish as though they were your sisters and brothers. It means saying the land is an old friend and an old friend your father knew, your people have always known. . . . To the Indian people our land is really our life."
Richard Nerysoo, Inuit

There is no universally agreed name for the peoples whose lives, conditions, and aspirations are featured in this book. The book describes them as first peoples, because their ancestors were the original inhabitants of their lands, since colonized by foreigners. Many territories continue to be so invaded. The book also calls them indigenous, a term widely accepted by the peoples themselves, and now adopted by the United Nations.

In 1500, the beginning of European expansion, most peoples lived on their original lands practising subsistence agriculture, hunting and gathering. Although large-scale migrations had taken place and civilizations had emerged and ebbed in other parts of the world, it was modern colonialism that forced the native inhabitants from their lands. Australian Aborigines, New Zealand Maoris, North and South American Indians, the indigenous peoples of northern and eastern Russia were, in large numbers, killed, assimilated, or pushed into marginal lands, where some already lived by choice. In Asia and Africa, where European settlement was on a smaller scale, artificial borders divided peoples or turned them into powerless minorities. First peoples are a legacy of colonialism, old and new.

First peoples have a strong sense of their own identity as unique peoples, with their own lands, languages, and cultures. They claim the right to

Origin of names? *The names indigenous peoples give themselves – Inuit, Saami, Kayapo, Maori, Hmong, and others – generally mean simply "people", and the names they give their territories often can be translated as "our land".*

The land is a part of who we are *In defending a sacred dreaming place from outside culture, these Aborigine boys in central Australia are holding on to the integrity of their way of life and their ancestral roots. This deep sense of belonging to the land is central to the identity of first peoples the world over.*

define what is meant by indigenous, and to be recognized as such by others. Some now live in cities, earning their livings as, for example, lawyers and community workers – or in many cases struggling to make ends meet; others retain a traditional way of life. But they are united in their desire to maintain their identity and yet be able to adapt and survive.

Indigenous societies often share a set of values, that are in marked contrast to Western priorities. Cree in Alberta, Quechua in the Peruvian highlands, Santal in the forests in Bihar, India, are all connected through their profound relationship with the land. First peoples seek to retain that respect for nature through a sustainable and co-operative way of life.

WHERE ARE FIRST PEOPLES?

There are 250 million indigenous peoples worldwide – 4 per cent of the global population – living in over 70 countries. And if the distinct indigenous peoples of Africa are included (not counted in figure because they do not fall within the strict definitions of indigenous used in this book), then that figure can be doubled. In most countries, indigenous peoples are a minority. In Brazil and Sweden fewer than 0.1 per cent are indigenous; in the USA, fewer than 0.5 per cent. But in Greenland they account for 90 per cent, in Bolivia 66 per cent, and in Peru 40 per cent of the population. The greatest numbers are concentrated in Asia – 86 million in China, 51 million in India – even though they make up only 7 per cent of the population. National borders have divided first peoples all over the world. The Inuit, for example, are subjects of the governments in Canada, Greenland, USA (Alaska), and USSR; the Fulani of West Africa extend across eight countries; the Papuans are the subjects of Indonesian rule

Canada and North America
3. Pacific Coast HAIDA, TLINGIT, KWAKIUTL, BELLA COOLA, TSIMSHIAN, NOOTKA
4. Central Canada CREE, METI, CHIPEWYAN, BLACKFOOT, DENE
5. Eastern Canada INNU, CREE, including JAMES BAY CREE
6. Canada/USA border MICMAC; The Six Nation Confederacy, or Haudenosaunee, comprising MOHAWK, ONEIDA, ONONDAGA, CAYUGA, SENECA, TUSCARORA
7. NW USA NEZ PERCE
8. SW USA NAVAJO, UTI, PUEBLO, including HOPI, KERES, ZUNI; DINE
9. Plains CROW, CHEYENNE, ARAPAHO, PAWNEE, COMANCHE, OGLALA SIOUX, SHOSHONE

Central America
10. Mexico Mayan descendants – LACANDON, YUCATEC; Aztec descendants – HUICHOL, TARAHUMARA, NAHUA, ZAPOTEC; also refugees
11. Guatemala, Belize MAYA including CHOL, CHUJ, KEKCHI, QUICHE; Nicaragua MISKITO, SUMU, RAMA; El Salvador, Honduras LENCA, PIPILE
12. Panama KUNA, GUAYMI

Arctic and Europe
1. Arctic INUIT (Eskimo) in Alaska, Canada, Greenland, and USSR. ALEUT, Alaska
2. Europe SAAMI in Norway, Sweden, Finland, and USSR

South America
13. Highland Peru, Bolivia, Ecuador, Colombian Highlands QUECHUA, AYMARA
14. Argentina, Chile MAPUCHE
15. Amazon Basin – Brazil TUKANO, XAVANTE, YANOMAMI, PARAKANA, KREEN-AKRORE, NAMBIKWARA, KAYAPO, MAKUXI, WAIMIRI-ATROARI; Amazon Basin – Ecuador, Bolivia, Peru, Colombia, Venezuela AMARAKAERI, AMUESHA, AGUARUNA, MATSIGENKA, YAGUA, SHIPIBO, TUKANO, PANARE, SANEMA, SECOYA, SHUAR, QUICHUA, GUAJIRO, YANESHA, WAORANI, UFAINA; Paraguay ACHE, AYOREO, GUARANI, TOBA-MASKOY; Guyana, French Guiana, Surinam ARAWAK, LAKONO, KALINJA, WAYANA, AKAWAIO

and their own Papua New Guinea government. Fourth World is a term used by the World Council of Indigenous Peoples (see p.178) to distinguish the way of life of indigenous peoples from those of the First (highly industrialized), Second (Socialist bloc) and Third (developing) worlds. The First, Second, and Third Worlds believe that *"the land belongs to the people"*; the Fourth World believes that *"the people belong to the land"*. The map below indicates regional concentrations of indigenous peoples. For more information, see Index of Peoples, pp. 181-5.

"The Fourth World is the name given to indigenous peoples descended from a country's aboriginal population and who today are completely or partly deprived of the right to their own territory and its riches. The peoples of the Fourth World have only limited influence or none at all in the national state to which they belong."
George Manuel, World Council of Indigenous Peoples

East Asia and USSR
32. China TIBETAN, UIGHUR
33. Mongolia MONGOLIAN
34. Japan AINU
35. USSR YUIT, KAZAKH, SAAMI, CHUKCHI, NEMET

South East Asia
26. Myanmar (Burma) KAREN, KACHIN, SHAN, CHIN
27. Thailand KAREN, HMONG, LISU
28. Malaysia PENAN, KAYAN, IBAN
29. Philippines KALINGA, IFUGAO, HANUNOO, BONTOC, BANGSA MORO
30. Indonesia – Kalimantan DAYAK; Lembata KEDANG; West Papua (Irian Jaya) WEST PAPUAN including ASMAT, DANI
31. Papua New Guinea including MAE-ENGA, DANI, TSEMBAGA

Africa
16. Sahara, Sahel TUAREG, FULANI
17. S. Sudan DINKA, NUER, SHILLUK
18. Angola, Botswana, Namibia SAN (Bushmen)
19. Kenya, Tanzania MAASAI
20. Ethiopia OROMO, SOMALI, TIGRAYAN, ERITREAN
21. Zaire, Cameroon, Central African Republic, Congo MBUTI, EFE, LESE

South Asia
22. India NAGA, SANTAL, GOND, KAMENG, LOHIT, DANDAMI
23. Afghanistan, Pakistan PATHAN
24. Sri Lanka VEDDA
25. Bangladesh CHITTAGONG HILL TRACT PEOPLES, including CHAKMA, MARMA, TRIPURA

Oceania
36. Australia ABORIGINES
37. New Zealand MAORIS
38. Pacific Islands KANAK, HAWAIIAN, TAHITIAN, CHAMORRO

RELATIONSHIP TO THE LAND

"Every part of the earth is sacred to my people. Every shining pine needle, every sandy shore, every mist in the dark woods, every clearing and humming insect is holy in the memory and experience of my people."
A Duwamish chief

For first peoples the land is the source of life – a gift from the creator that nourishes, supports, and teaches. Although indigenous peoples vary widely in their customs, culture, and impact on the land, all consider the Earth like a parent and revere it accordingly. "Mother Earth" is the centre of the universe, the core of their culture, the origin of their identity as a people. She connects them with their past (as the home of the ancestors), with the present (as provider of their material needs), and with the future (as the legacy they hold in trust for their children and grandchildren). In this way, indigenousness carries with it a sense of belonging to a place. In the words of Aborigine Pat Dodson *"land cannot be given or taken away. We belong to the land; our birth does not sever the cord of life which comes from the land. Our spirituality, our culture and our social life depend on it."* At the heart of this deep bond is a perception, an awareness, that all of life – mountains, rivers, skies, animals, plants, insects, rocks, people – are inseparably interconnected. Material and spiritual worlds are woven together in one complex web, all living things imbued with a sacred meaning. This living sense of connectedness that grounds indigenous peoples in the soil has all but disappeared among city dwellers – the cause of much modern alienation and despair.

The idea that the land can be owned, that it can belong to someone even when left unused, uncared for, or uninhabited is foreign to indigenous peoples. As Sealth, a Duwamish chief, asks *"How can you buy or sell the land – the warmth of the land? The idea is strange to us. We do not own the freshness of the air or the sparkle of the water. How can you buy them from us?"*. In the developed world, land is in

"The Earth is the foundation of Indigenous Peoples, it is the seat of spirituality, the fountain from which our cultures and languages flourish. The Earth is our historian, the keeper of events and the bones of our forefathers. Earth provides us with food, medicine, shelter and clothing. It is the source of our independence, it is our Mother. We do not dominate her; we must harmonize with her."
Hayden Burgess, native Hawaiian

"In the Indian the spirit of the land is still vested; it will be until other men are able to divine and meet its rhythm. Men must be born and reborn to belong. Their bodies must be formed of the dust of their forefathers' bones." North American Indian

"One has only to develop a relationship with a certain place, where the land knows you and experience that the trees, the Earth and Nature are extending their love and light to you to know there is so much we can receive from the Earth to fill our hearts and souls."
Inti Melasquez, Inca Shaman

Balancing the opposites *This painted hide – thought to be part of an ancient altar – depicts the holistic viewpoint of the Pueblo Indians. Male and female fertility symbols, night and day, sun and moon, black and white, God and human are the dualities that make up the whole of nature.*

Seeing life in nature *Algonquin photographer Greg Stevens reveals animal and spirit forms living within rocks, trees, and driftwood. "Raven the Nest Robber" (below) talks of the need to hunt to survive.*

The source of all life *The Earth is frequently depicted as a symbol of abundance in indigenous art. In many cultures, particularly in North America, corn – the fruit of the Earth – represents fertility, the subject chosen by Hopi artist, Waldo Nootzka (left).*

Temples to the Earth *Indigenous cultures have often created images in the landscape that reflect their understanding of the natural and symbolic worlds. The Ohio earthwork (below) of the serpent and the egg is a universal symbol of fertility and the transformation of matter within nature. The spiral in the serpent's tail is an image of wisdom and the life force inherent in the Earth. Such earth sculptures are an expression of the deep respect for the Earth.*

the hands of private individuals, corporate investors, or the state and can be disposed of at the will of the owner. For indigenous peoples land is held collectively for the community (though competition between communities, and with outsiders, for rights of use, has sometimes lead to conflict). According to indigenous law, humankind can never be more than a trustee of the land, with a collective responsibility to preserve it.

The predominant Western world view is that nature must be studied, dissected, and mastered, and progress measured by the ability to extract secrets and wealth from the Earth. The First World has dominated the Earth to enrich itself in many cases. First peoples do not consider the land as merely an economic resource. Their ancestral lands are literally the source of life, and their distinct ways of life are developed and defined in relationship to the environment around them. First peoples are people of the land. This difference has often lead to misunderstandings. Many have assumed that indigenous peoples have no sense of territory because they do not necessarily physically demarcate their lands. But all first peoples know the extent of their lands, and they know how the land, water, and other resources need to be shared. They understand only too well that to harm the land is to destroy ourselves, since we are all part of the same organism. They sense, too, that the Earth will survive long after human beings. *"When the last red man has vanished from the Earth, and the memory is only the shadow of a cloud moving across the prairie, these shores and forests will still hold the spirits of my people, for they love this Earth as the newborn loves its mother's heartbeat."* Sealth, a Duwamish chief

"Traditional people, still in harmony with the world around them, do not isolate themselves from other living things, nor consider one creature superior to another." Californian Indian

"We think the land is there for everyone to use, the way our hand is there, a part of our own body." Buffalo Tiger, Miccosukee

"The grass and trees are our flesh, the animals are our flesh." Susie Tutcho, Fort Franklin

"Man is an aspect of nature, and nature itself is a manifestation of primordial religion. Even the word 'religion' makes an unnecessary separation, and there is no word for it in the Indian tongues. Nature is the 'Great Mysterious', the 'religion before religion', the profound intuitive apprehension of the true nature of existence attained by sages of all epochs, everywhere on Earth, the whole universe is sacred, man is the whole universe, and the religious ceremony is life itself, the miraculous common acts of every day." Peter Matthiessen, Indian Country

"We Indian people are not supposed to say, this land is mine. We only use it. It is the white man who buys land and puts a fence around it. Indians are not supposed to do that, because the land belongs to all Indians, it belongs to God, as you call it. The land is a part of our body, and we are a part of the land." Buffalo Tiger, Miccosukee

DESERT STOREHOUSE
The San of the Kalahari

Even the desert can support a human population. An apparently inhospitable land of grass and bush-covered sand is home to 62,000 San, or Bushmen, of the Kalahari Desert in southern Africa. The San hunt animals and gather plants over a vast area. Their way of life has provided liberty, leisure, and food security out of reach of the more "advanced" areas of Africa.

Today, only a few thousand San Bushmen still follow their original way of life. Traditionally, they live and move in groups of 20 or less, camping for only a few weeks in one place and hunting and gathering over an area of up to 600sq km (230sq miles) around the camp.

The San way of life is integrated with their environment. The small size of San communities enables them to continue their traditional hunting and gathering without depleting the land's resources. At least 80 types of animal are hunted in their region. Their knowledge of the area and of the animals and plants, and their co-operation with neighbouring San enable them to procure a sufficient food supply. By owning few possessions, and sharing those they have, the San enjoy an unrestricted freedom of movement.

Finely attuned to desert life, the San have a strong sense of survival. In times of drought the women cease to conceive; when hunting they take care not to hurt females and young of the prey species; they make fires with the minimum amount of wood; they store water in ostrich shells; and they use almost every part of the animals they hunt.

Today, an estimated 62,000 San – 25,000 in Botswana, 29,000 in Namibia, and 8000 in Angola – occupy a small area of the Kalahari. Encroaching cattle ranchers from Botswana and recent fighting in Namibia have made the San way of life difficult to maintain.

The first artist *Rock paintings supply evidence of the San at least 10,000 years ago. Men are the hunters; women gather small animals and plants, and report signs of game in the area to the men.*

Water storage *Water supplies determine the animal population and, in turn, the size of a San community. Rainfall is low and unreliable, producing occasional water holes and rivers, around which the animals congregate. The San store small quantities of water for themselves in ostrich shells, sometimes burying them underground for later use.*

LAYERS OF MEANING
The Sanema of Venezuela

The Sanema live in one of the last relatively isolated reaches of rainforest in South America, and rely entirely on the forest and their gardens for a living. The vigorous way of life required to manage the rainforest is only made easy by the Sanema's intimate knowledge of their environment. In return, the land sustains them on every level – physically, socially and spiritually.

The Sanema have developed a system of agriculture that is undemanding on the soil. They plant crops, such as cassava, bananas, cocoyams, and plantains, that grow easily in the nitrogen-poor soils. And they move often to allow the exhausted soil to recover. The low-protein garden produce is usually complemented by meat, obtained by hunting with bows and arrows within an 8-km (5-mile) radius of their main village. Integral to the Sanema economy are long periods when they abandon their gardens and trek in the forest, setting up temporary shelters as far as 25km (15 miles) from the village, in order to hunt and collect forest foods, which minimizes the burden on any one area of land.

Leadership is minimal and, where there is conflict, villages may break up into smaller groups, thus reducing the pressure on the land. Sanema children are fiercely individualist, yet they are imbued from an early age with a deep sense of the need to exchange and share. Selfishness is considered an immoral act.

The Sanema interpret nature – from the calls of birds to the play of light on leaves – in both practical and metaphysical ways. Their life is rich in symbols, resembling the richness of their world.

Channels of communication
Sanema people openly express their feelings and share their concerns with each other (right). Speech, however, is but one form of communication with others and with the environment. Animal calls, plays of light, seed down, are not only physical phenomena, but complex symbolic messages from the forest.

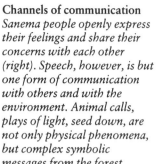

Sparing the land *A balanced relationship to the land affords the Sanema a balanced diet. Crops that draw the minimum from the soil, such as bananas, yams, and cassava (left) provide a dependable source of calories. And the forest yields sufficient protein, vitamins, and minerals from game, fruits, crustaceans, insects and shell reptiles. Villages move often, allowing soil and forest to recover naturally.*

VALUING THE NATURAL WORLD
Inuit in two worlds

The inhospitable Arctic, with temperatures as low as -50°C (-58°F), snow blizzards, and little winter daylight, is home to approximately 100,000 Inuit (formerly known as Eskimo) and has been for over 7000 years. In the past the Inuit thrived on hunting and fishing. Now they must keep one foot in today's world, the other firmly in their traditional culture.

Most Inuit now work for wages – fewer than 800 of Greenland's 42,000 Inuit still make a living solely from hunting. Even these often use skidoos and rifles, replacing dog teams, spears, and harpoons.

Traditional methods of survival in this area have produced a unique culture. First, Inuit dependence on animals and the land has led to a respect for both, for without them there is no future for their people. Second, in the highly mobile hunting culture, where wind, weather, and animal movements change constantly, decisions must be made quickly, and individual decisions are given a high regard. Third, the Inuit cannot be attached to one piece of land: as hunters home is everywhere and nowhere at the same time.

The cycle of animal life dictates the pattern of traditional Inuit activity. In spring they hunt seals and nesting birds. Summer brings other sea mammals, including the walrus; caribou are hunted in autumn and fishing takes place all year.

While the Inuit welcome the greater comforts brought by the mineral boom in the Arctic, they foresee a breakdown in their traditional relationship with nature. As one Inuit said: *"We draw our identity as a people from our relationship to the land and to the sea and to the resources. This is a spiritual relationship."*

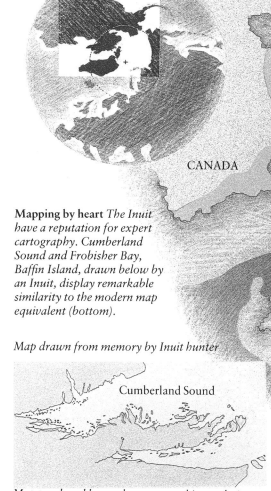

CANADA

Mapping by heart *The Inuit have a reputation for expert cartography. Cumberland Sound and Frobisher Bay, Baffin Island, drawn below by an Inuit, display remarkable similarity to the modern map equivalent (bottom).*

Map drawn from memory by Inuit hunter

Cumberland Sound

Map produced by modern map-making techniques

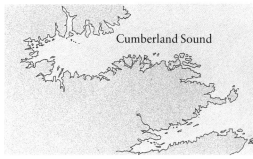

Cumberland Sound

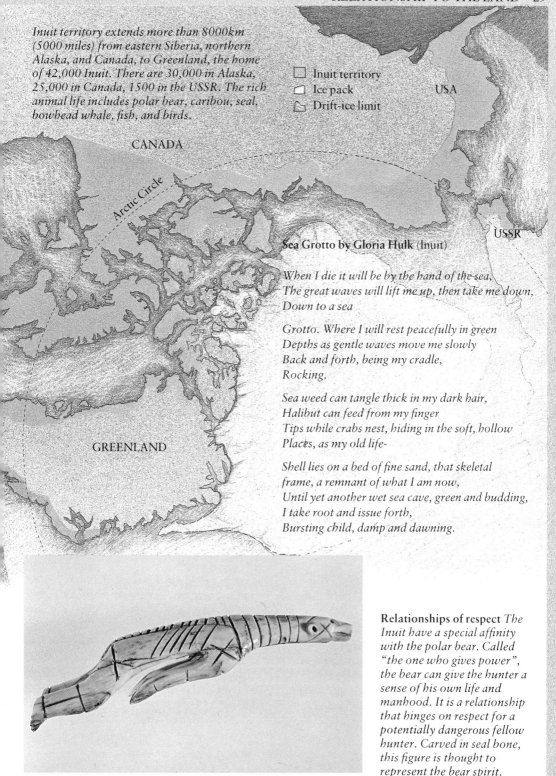

Inuit territory extends more than 8000km (5000 miles) from eastern Siberia, northern Alaska, and Canada, to Greenland, the home of 42,000 Inuit. There are 30,000 in Alaska, 25,000 in Canada, 1500 in the USSR. The rich animal life includes polar bear, caribou, seal, bowhead whale, fish, and birds.

☐ Inuit territory
◻ Ice pack
◿ Drift-ice limit

USA

CANADA

Arctic Circle

USSR

GREENLAND

Sea Grotto by Gloria Hulk (Inuit)

When I die it will be by the hand of the sea,
The great waves will lift me up, then take me down,
Down to a sea

Grotto. Where I will rest peacefully in green
Depths as gentle waves move me slowly
Back and forth, being my cradle,
Rocking.

Sea weed can tangle thick in my dark hair,
Halibut can feed from my finger
Tips while crabs nest, hiding in the soft, hollow
Places, as my old life-

Shell lies on a bed of fine sand, that skeletal
frame, a remnant of what I am now,
Until yet another wet sea cave, green and budding,
I take root and issue forth,
Bursting child, damp and dawning.

Relationships of respect *The Inuit have a special affinity with the polar bear. Called "the one who gives power", the bear can give the hunter a sense of his own life and manhood. It is a relationship that hinges on respect for a potentially dangerous fellow hunter. Carved in seal bone, this figure is thought to represent the bear spirit.*

GUIDED BY NATURE
Master navigators of the South Seas

Traditionally the Pacific Islanders sail ocean voyages of 500km (300 miles) or more – for food gathering, trading, and social or political visits – guided only by the wind, waves, stars, and birds, and protected by the gods of the sea. Even since modernization, many islanders still use their traditional navigational skills.

In South Sea culture, the canoe is the mother; the master navigator, or *Palu*, is the father, and the crew are the children. The night before a long voyage the crew have a feast and separate from their families. The next morning they leave the island with farewells and, once at sea, throw away their feelings about the land to please the ocean spirits and concentrate only on the ocean and their eventual destination.

By day the mariners set course by the position of the sun, the set of the currents, and the behaviour of the swells, and observe the species of birds and fish, the shifts in the wind, and the colour of the waves. At night they follow the stars. If a squall threatens they blow a conch to ward it off. The *Palu* draws on the goodwill of the spirits as well as the knowledge of past generations to guide his boat.

The land and the women provide the raw material for these voyages. With the hull of a canoe carved from a breadfruit tree specially grown for the purpose, the boat builder adds ropes and binding from coconut husks and sails from pandanus trees. The women, who own the land titles, prepare breadfruit biscuits for the journey, and on the men's return cook turtle, octopus and other protein-rich sea foods.

Spirit protection *Despite modernization many Pacific peoples retain the skills to cross vast expanses of sea with few provisions and only the guidance of the wind, waves, stars, and birds. A safe voyage requires the protection of the gods of the sea, and the rich cosmology of the indigenous Pacific Islanders ensures this. Each group of islands has it own myths, which at the same time explain their origin and guarantee a safe passage. Appropriate carvings, paintings, and launching ceremonies add to their protection.*

The means to travel *Single-outrigger canoes are found throughout the Pacific; smaller ones, usually with paddles, are for fishing; larger sailing boats for voyages. Each group of islands has its own design. The outrigger prevents these cata-maran-style boats from over-turning. Boats can reach 40km (25 miles) per hour, but, as one Palu says, "only the sea knows if a canoe will be fast".*

The Pacific Ocean covers an area of 180 million sq km (70 million sq miles) – one-third of the surface of the planet. It is home to 10 million people: Asians, Europeans, and three distinct indigenous linguistic and cultural groups – Melanesians, Polynesians, and Micronesians.

KNOWLEDGE OF NATURE

"I am trying to save the knowledge that the forests and this planet are alive, to give it back to you who have lost the understanding." Paulinho Paiakan

A leader of the Kayapo of Brazil, Paulinho Paiakan, calls the forest "our university". And indigenous knowledge is held, not only in nature, but in the minds of elders, shamans, and medicine men. It is a wisdom passed down orally from generation to generation and if the chain is broken, the knowledge is lost for ever.

In many parts of the world indigenous societies classify soils, climate, plant, and animal species and recognize their special characteristics. Indigenous peoples have words for plants and insects that have not yet been identified by the world's botanists and entomologists. The Hanunoo people of the Philippines, for example, distinguish 1600 plant species in their forest, 400 more than scientists working in the same area. Of the estimated 250,000 to 500,000 plant species in the world, more than 85 per cent are in environments that are the traditional homes of indigenous people. Nearly 75 per cent of 121 plant-derived prescription drugs used worldwide were discovered following leads from indigenous medicine. Globally, indigenous peoples use 3000 different species of plant to control fertility alone. The Kallaywayas, wandering healers of Bolivia, make use of 600 medicinal herbs; traditional healers in Southeast Asia may employ as many as 6500 plants for drugs. Almost all trees and many plants have a place in medicinal lore.

Some scientists now believe that indigenous knowledge may help them to discover important new cures for diseases such as AIDS and cancer. Many developing countries realize the potential for indigenous medicine. It is locally available, culturally acceptable, and cheaper than imported drugs. The AMETRA project in Peru, for example, founded by a shaman of the Shipibo, is teaching health workers to use plant remedies alongside pharmaceutical drugs. Fears are growing, however,

Hunter and hunted *Many Inuit carvings reflect the importance of caribou.* "A person is born with animals. He has to eat animals. That is why the animals and a person are just like one."

"Migration with the reindeer has been an important factor in the development of Saami culture. The wandering life is a life of freedom. There are no chains binding us to the same place. New landscapes and new perspectives also liberate the mind and thoughts." Nils-Aslak Valkeapaa, Saami artist

Nature's knowledge *This Amazonian plant,* Anadenanthera peregrina *(right) protects itself against extinction with "barnacles" on its bark and hallucinogens in its fruits. Brazilian Indians respect its survival mechanisms and extract small quantities of hallucinogens to use in religious practices, for enlightenment and "protection."*

that indigenous knowledge will be exploited to enrich outsiders, not to enhance the living standards of indigenous peoples.

Indigenous treatments are based on a deep knowledge of the healing process. A medicine man or woman approaches each individual in a unique way, working on the relationship between body and spirit, and calling up the patient's own healing powers. He or she also knows not only the spiritual power of a medicinal plant but its physical properties – at what time of day and place to collect it, what quantities to give and how often. A plant may, for example, have higher concentrations of the medicinal ingredient at dawn.

Indigenous knowledge of nature has ensured the survival of many peoples in fragile habitats. But it is a knowledge centred not on exploitation but on the harmony of the natural world. All flora and fauna have a place in an ordered universe made up of humankind, nature, and spirits. And indigenous cultures help to protect the natural world from destruction through religion and rituals. Animals are commonly held in respect and their numbers maintained, often through careful management. Those following the Bishnoi religion in India, for example, have survived many droughts because they will not kill an animal or a tree. They breed cattle selectively, monitor the feeding of their camels, and live on milk, yoghurt, and a few cultivated crops. Many peoples have developed a detailed understanding of animal behaviour. Those living in tropical forests, for example, recognize that where two different ecological zones meet, the hunting is more productive. Many even grow crops or trees to attract certain animals and increase their numbers.

"There are no such things as natural landscapes in Amazonia, the forest has been moulded by native peoples. The monuments of their civilization are not cities and temples, but the natural environment itself." Darrell Posey

"With the extinction of each indigenous group, the world loses millennia of accumulated knowledge about life in, and adaptation to, tropical ecosystems."

"When Indians referred to animals as 'people' – just a different sort of person from Man – they were not being quaint. Nature to them was a community of such 'people' for whom they had a great deal of genuine regard and with whom they had a contractual relationship to protect one another's interests and to fulfill their mutual needs. Man and Nature, in short, was jointed by compact – not by ethical ties – a compact predicated on mutual esteem. This was the essence of the traditional land relationship." Ojibway magazine

"Now your way of life is no longer working, and so you are interested in our way. But if we tell you our way, then it will be polluted, we will have no medicine, and we will be destroyed as well as you." Buffalo Tiger, Miccasukee Indian

"Indigenous knowledge is important, extremely important to humanity. It's a new way of thinking, a new model. It's an alternative model, which we can in fact learn from and must learn from if we're going to stop this senseless destruction of the Amazon." Darrell Posey, ethnobotanist

ANIMALS AS EQUALS
The Tukano of Brazil

In recognizing their need for animals, whether it be for food, transport, clothing, or shelter, many indigenous peoples develop a respect for living creatures. Seen as equals, animals and their animal spirits are enmeshed in their lives: a detailed knowledge and understanding of animal behaviour enables them to seek a balance both within the animal population and between humans and animals.

In Brazil's Uaupes basin of the northwest Amazon rainforest, the river contains little organic matter on which the fish can feed. The Tukano Indians, however, have mastered the art of sustainable fishing. They derive most of their protein from fish in the river, by careful management of the fragile balance between the fish and the food they eat.

Cultivation and deforestation along the river banks are forbidden: this area belongs to the fish, according to Tukano beliefs, and the Tukano have no rights over it. The stretches of river that can be fished are also carefully laid down: in one community two-thirds of the river is out of bounds to fishermen. This is a reserve area, the resting place of ancestors, not to be disturbed. In practice, these areas provide spawning grounds that preserve the fish population. If they ignore the taboo, the Tukano believe the ancestors of the fish will take one child for every fish taken. In this way the river stock is never depleted.

The belief that humans and fish are equal and interdependent is fundamental to the Tukano: their life depends on it.

Maximizing their knowledge
The Uaupes River floods twice a year and nutrients leach into the water from the forest margins. These floods increase the level of organic matter in the river, on which the fish feed. Tukano fishermen use a long bow and poison-covered arrows and fish only in the permitted areas.

FRUITS OF THE FOREST
The Kayapo of Brazil

Indigenous rainforest peoples throughout the Amazon have developed a sophisticated system of forest management: they not only make use of an enormous variety of plant life, but cultivate gardens in a highly organized way. The Kayapo of Brazil practise seed selection, fertilization of the soil, and crop rotation. They complement their agriculture with hunting, gathering, and fishing. In this way they benefit from a very wide range of nourishment while regrowth and replenishment in the forest ensure food for their future.

The Kayapo gather about 250 types of wild fruit, hundreds of tubers, nuts, and leaves, and at least 650 medicinal plants (see p. 32). One village may clear 500km (315 miles) of trails, each about 2.5m (8ft) wide, for gathering expeditions in the forest that last several days, or even months. The trails are planted with sweet potatoes, yams, fruits, and other edible plants.

Garden clearings contain a wide range of trees and plants, of various sizes and with different rates of growth. Some are harvested after several months or even several years. Others will continue to provide for up to 40 years and are visited long after the village has abandoned its site. The gardens are planted in complementary groupings – "friends who grow together" as the Kayapo say. Some plants are known to be companions; others secrete toxins underground that are harmful to certain neighbours. A variety of banana tree, the habitat of wasps, is grown as hedging to keep out foliage-eating ants. The range and number of crops help ensure against any failures in the harvest.

Managing the land *Using long bows and arrows, small groups of Kayapo hunt animals such as peccary, paca and tapir. Several distinct ecological zones are inhabited by the Kayapo, including savannah land and forest. The Kayapo have re-established "islands" of fertile land in open savannah by transporting rotting vegetation and the rich soil from ant and termite nests to sites that collect water. As the soil regains its fertility, the Kayapo sow trees and plants, sometimes over an area as large as 10 hectares.*

Family cultivation *Kayapo women clear gardens outside the village, where they plant crops including manioc, tobacco, and sweet potatoes. Careful cultivators, the Kayapo select plants with special qualities, such as flavour and resistance to disease. Each family of Kayapo is responsible for the culture and improvement of a specific, cultivated plant.*

NATURE'S PHARMACY
Medicinal plants in India

Indigenous peoples work on body and mind together to help cure illness. Medicinal plants are used to treat the spiritual origins of disease as well as the physical symptoms. The vast knowledge of such plants is now beginning to be acknowledged by the rest of the world. So is the role played by indigenous people as custodians of the world's genetic heritage.

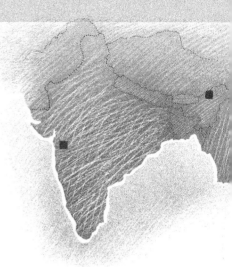

A botanical survey of India revealed that tribal peoples of the northeast use plant drugs to cure fevers, bronchitis, blood and skin diseases, eye infections, lung and spleen ulcers, diabetes, and high blood pressure. Knowledge of their use is passed on by the "vaiyas", Indian herbal medicine doctors. In a single area of 277 sq km (107 sq miles) 210 types of medicinal plants have been found.

The Kameng and Lohit peoples in Arunachal Pradesh, crush a bulb of *Fritillaria cirrhosa* to a paste to relieve muscle pains. Soviet research has now confirmed the presence of a chemical similar to cocaine in a related *Fritillaria* plant that brings relief to muscular pain.

Growing evidence of plant-based contraception is available among many tribal peoples. Worldwide, over 3000 plants are employed for contraceptive use. In the Karjat tribal area of Maharashtra, near the west coast of India, a native herb taken twice a year is said to be effective.

The Karjat study concludes that traditional health practices can provide up to half the local primary health needs. Enlightened health-care workers are beginning to re-introduce traditional plant remedies where allopathic drugs have become commonplace. Properly studied and recorded, this traditional knowledge could revolutionize the world of medicine.

Using the knowledge *At least 75% of our plant-based prescription drugs in the Western world are derived from medicinal plants from tribal areas. It takes on average 7 years to develop a drug that meets the standards of modern Western medicine, from plants identified as having medicinal use by local tribespeople. This clinic (left) in West Bengal is dispensing traditional, plant-based drugs, continuing long-established patterns of medical care. In the picture below tribal people harvest a crop of ginger.*

RESOURCE MANAGEMENT

*"When we Indians kill meat, we eat it
all up. . . . When we build houses, we
make little holes. When we burn grass
for grasshoppers, we don't ruin things.
We shake down acorns and pinenuts.
We don't chop down the trees."* Wintu
Indian, California

The industrial world is facing an ecological crisis.
Yet few industrial economists would admit they
could learn from first peoples. Their economies are
often called primitive, their technology dismissed as
"Stone Age", and most governments assume they
can benefit only from salaried employment.

Yet these traditional ways of life have proved
highly durable. Hunting and fishing have allowed
the Inuit to survive in the Arctic; nomadic
pastoralism provides a livelihood for people in the
arid Sahelian region of Africa; shifting cultivation
has sustained hundreds of distinct cultures in the
fragile ecosystem in the Amazon and the forests of
Southeast Asia. Non-indigenous peoples have not
been able to survive in these extreme conditions
without destroying the balance of the ecosystem.

The key to this success is sustainability.
Indigenous peoples today use the resources
available without depleting them. They use their
intimate knowledge of plants, soils, animals,
climate, and seasons, not to exploit nature but to
co-exist alongside it. This involves careful
management, control of population, the use of small
quantities but a wide diversity of plants and
animals, small surpluses, and minimum wastage.
Plants provide food, medicines, pesticides, poisons,
building materials; animals provide meat, clothes,
string, implements, oil. Even when making pots out
of earth, this sense of economy prevails. *"When we
make pottery, we are very careful, and do not waste
anything, because we know where it comes from."*

Although not associated with economy of effort,
many traditional ways of life – particularly hunting
and gathering – allow for extensive leisure time. In
the rainy season, for example, the San of the

Learning the trade *Fishing is
the chief economic activity and
source of food for several million coastal and island dwellers, as well as many river
peoples. Children of the Caroline Islanders in Micronesia
(above) become skilled fishers
and sailors at any early age.*

Living off the land *Some 20
million people live by herding
animals, mainly in the Sahel,
East Africa and central Asia.
No more than 50 societies still
survive by hunting and gathering in the forests, tundra, and
bush. Around 50 million people live by shifting cultivation –
a sustainable practice when
densities are not too high.*

Subsistence agriculture   Hunting and gathering

Shifting cultivation   Nomadic herding

Kalahari would spend two to three days hunting and gathering vegetables, leaving four or five days in camp talking, singing, dancing, and telling stories. How many in the industrialized countries could flourish on a two- or three-day working week?

The economic life of indigenous people is based not on competition but on co-operation, for survival is only possible when the community works together. Most small-scale indigenous societies have elaborate systems for sharing food, possessions, and ritualizing conflict. And, although largely self-sufficient, many groups have developed mutually beneficial trading relationships. In India, for example, shifting cultivators in the forest have traded with their settled neighbours for centuries. Economic practices are also intricately linked with religious as well as social values. The Karen in Thailand will look for good omens when selecting a field for clearing; a San will seek divination before setting off on a hunt; and the thrift common to all indigenous peoples is as much an expression of care and courtesy toward the natural world as a practical means of survival.

Indigenous forms of economy cannot, of course, satisfy the needs of a burgeoning world population now nearing 6 billion. But the knowledge and, especially, the values of the peoples practising them are vital. The scientific community has recently begun research into indigenous skills in resource management. But it is, above all wisdom that is needed in Western culture – we all need to learn respect for the Earth, conservation of resources, equitable distribution of wealth, harmony, balance, and modest co-operation. In 1928 Gandhi wrote: *"God forbid that India should ever take to industrialism after the manner of the West . . . It would strip the world bare like locusts."* Today all nations are set on a self-destructive economic path. The lesson from indigenous peoples is to live with, not against, the only world we have.

"An Innu hunter's prestige comes not from the wealth he accumulates but from what he gives away. When a hunter kills caribou or other game he shares with everyone else in the camp." Daniel Ashini, Innu

"The young people . . . get out into the bush whenever they can. We are Indians just like our fathers and grandfathers and just like our children and grandchildren will be." Richard Nerysoo, Inuit

"Whatever kind of food I wanted, if I wanted caribou I'd go up in the mountains; if I wanted coloured fox, I went up in the mountain; in the Delta I get mink, muskrat; but I never make a big trapper. I just get enough for my own use the coming year. Next year the animals all going to be there anyway, that's my bank. The same way all over where I travelled." Bertram Pokiak, Inuit

CIRCULATION OF WEALTH
Potlatch of the Pacific Northwest

The distribution of wealth is central to the social systems of all peoples, and many indigenous peoples honour their social and ritual obligations toward kin or community by displaying generosity. In some cultures a person's prestige and standing is determined by how much can be given away. Among Pacific coast Americans this is known as the "potlatch".

Potlatch takes place whenever anyone undergoes a significant personal change, such as puberty, marriage, accession to chiefdom, or death. It is based on the idea that all wealth, material or symbolic, must circulate; it honours non-acquisitiveness, generosity, and redistribution of wealth through exchange. When ritual privileges are publicly transmitted to the next generation, prestigious objects are given away, accompanied by feasts, speeches, songs, and dancing.

Traditionally the potlatches were a means of affirming social and political prerogatives as well as placing obligations on friends, strengthening kinship ties and village solidarity. They could also end hostilities and re-establish good relations.

During the colonial period potlatch was seen as subversive and was outlawed, in the hope that it would disappear. But even with the majority of indigenous peoples of the Pacific coast (the Tlingit, Tsimshian, Haida, Kwakiutl, Nootka, and Bella Coola) active in the modern economy, they continue to adhere to a principle of the perpetual circulation of wealth. This sets them apart from the dominant society and enables them to assert their cultural identity. They place tribal membership above their role as citizens of modern Canada or America.

Haida copper plaque *Plaques were used as units of wealth, representing the value of the number of blankets given away at a potlatch ceremony. By being displayed at several pot-latches, plaques acquired the value of several thousand blankets. Many of them were named and decorated with crest figures. This one has beaver's incisor teeth and a scaly tail, which identify it as a Haida copper.*

SUSTAINABLE CULTIVATION
The Karen of Thailand

Shifting cultivation, or swidden (sometimes called "slash and burn"), is a sustainable economic system that need not harm the environment. It is the most commonly practised system among indigenous peoples of Asia and lowland Latin America, providing them with a high degree of economic independence and cultural integrity. Given sufficient land and low population density, it is a highly successful way of using the forest. The Karen of Thailand practise this system.

The economy of the largely uncontacted Karen people is based almost exclusively on subsistence dry rice production. An area is cleared of trees, undergrowth is burned, rice planted and later harvested. Each year a new site is chosen and the cycle takes seven years to return to the site first cleared. The system permits regeneration of the forest and thin tropical soils, and does not expose the steep slopes to heavy rains, which would eventually wash away the soil in a fixed-field system.

Money has virtually no place in a Karen community. If a village has enough food it is prosperous. When villagers say "we have enough rice", it means not simply that they will survive, but that they have everything they need. If, however, shifting cultivation is unable to provide for the entire needs of a village, the people grow chili or bamboo shoots, or they may collect and sell honey or other forest produce. Nearly all the income raised is used to buy rice.

"Depart all you evil spirits. We are going to work here for our food. To get sustenance for our wife and children. Let no sickness come upon us. We are going to work until it is finished." A man addresses the spirits before cultivation begins

Village life *Although many villages suffer periodic rice shortages, the Karen are self-sufficient and economically autonomous. They hunt, fish, gather vegetables, and where the village is long established, plant fruit trees. The forest also provides materials for house building. In addition, villagers keep chickens or pigs, and some own or part-own buffaloes, or occasionally an elephant.*

HUNTER-GATHERERS IN ZAIRE
The Mbuti pygmies

Modern hunting and gathering involves co-operation and the formation of economic relationships with other groups. In northeastern Ituri, a tropical rainforest in Zaire, a mutually supportive economic relationship has been developed between the Efe, a group of Mbuti "pygmies" who are semi-nomadic hunter-gatherers, and the Lese, a group of shifting cultivators. This relationship may have been in existence for more than a thousand years.

The Efe trade forest products, such as meat, honey, fish, wild yams, nuts, building materials, poisoned arrows, fibres for weaving mats and baskets, and medicinal plants, for the Lese's garden crops. So the Lese make a substantial contribution to the Efe's vegetable diet. The Lese are also masters of ironwork and pottery and provide the Efe with machetes, arrow heads, knives, cooking pots, and all kinds of containers. In addition the Efe work temporarily for the Lese, helping with clearing, planting, weeding, and harvesting. The Lese try to make the Efe dependent on them so that they can monopolize resources and civilize the Efe. For their part, the Efe believe that the relationship is to their advantage. They receive food and are represented by the Lese in dealings with the state authorities.

Since the 1950s the area has received an influx of settlers, mostly farmers growing cash crops who do not recognize the traditional relations between Efe and Lese. In addition the regional administration is trying to settle the Efe and make them plant crops and raise lifestock. They use threats, arrests, and police harassment. The Efe response has been to avoid contact and maintain their relationship with the Lese.

Hunting with bows and arrows
The Efe are renowned archers. During a hunt several men spread out in a semicircle over a wide terrain. By using cries and songs, they excite their hunting dogs, frightening the animals in front of them toward a fixed point, where the hunters are waiting. Antelope kills can be up to 45kg (99lb) in weight.

Gathering forest produce *A group of Efe women and children cook and eat what they have found in the forest. The most common type of hunting is described by the Kingwana word "tembea". This means to take a walk or wander about. The Efe wander with the intention of getting something, yet they will not necessarily know at the outset what they are looking for.*

RESPECTING THE FRAGILE LAND
The Tuareg of West Africa

Nomadic pastoralism is a successful form of animal husbandry carried out in extensive areas with harsh climates. These lands are often considered useless by others. The success of this type of pastoralism depends on the flexibility and mobility of the herders themselves, and on their deep knowledge and efficient management of the environment.

Pastoral economies are highly efficient. Recent research shows that the ecological efficiency of traditional pastoralists can often be as great, or greater than, the intensive ranches of industrialized countries. Domestic animals convert wild vegetation into milk and meat, and provide wool and hides. Manure is an important byproduct.

Nomadic pastoralists live in places so arid that they cannot be inhabited all year round, such as the driest savannas and desert edges of northern Africa, and the mountains and deserts of western and central Asia. In these desolate places, nomadic pastoralists are the landscape's sole human inhabitants. Because of the severity of the environments, households usually move in seasonal cycles that take them from dry- to wet-season pastures. Such movements are governed by precise rules. Nomadic pastoralists have traditional land tenure systems of great sophistication and animals represent wealth, both symbolically and socially. Water and grazing rights are the shared heritage of the tribe or community.

Continuous movement *In the short West African rains, Tuaregs move up into the desert to make use of the ephemeral grasses. As the dry season advances, they withdraw into more permanent grazing close to water. Continuous movement allows vegetation to re-establish itself, and the water sources and grazing lands to replenish.*

Temporary homes *Tuareg households may have camels herded far from home on the desert edge, and a mixed flock of sheep and goats around the camp. The camels provide milk and transport, with an occasional animal sold when major purchases have to be made. Sheep and goats also give milk, are sometimes eaten, or sold.*

SOCIAL RELATIONSHIPS

"In traditional Aboriginal society no one person was more important than another – all were parts of a whole. Growth and stature were measured by contribution, participation and accountability." Pat Dodson, Aborigine

Social cohesion has been the key to survival for many indigenous cultures. Food gathering and hunting depend on mutual support and co-operation, and disharmony within a part of the group is dangerous to the whole. In many cultures men and women have developed complementary, if not equal, roles; political decisions are arrived at by consensus in many cultures, and other social arrangements that benefit the entire community have often been incorporated into indigenous cultural traditions.

Marriage, for example, is an integral part of the social system – political, economic, and spiritual – in many indigenous societies. Among the Nuer of southern Sudan a marriage is an alliance between two lineages. Those who give away a woman who will bear children for the lineage receive cattle as compensation. In Thailand, a Hmong groom must pay a high dowry, but in return the wife becomes a member of the husband's clan under the direct authority of the household. Marriage can also ensure political stability for the community (by regulating exchange between groups), and continuing harmony with the spirit world. For essentially religious reasons, marriage may be prohibited between a man and woman of the same kin group; in other societies it can only take place within the kin group. The notion of marriage as a relationship founded only on the bond of romantic love is rarely, if ever, seen in traditional societies.

The nuclear family, too, is a rare concept. A complex interweaving of lineage, clan, and family connections means that most individuals are related to each other – a tradition that fosters the sense of belonging to the group, and of the need to share.

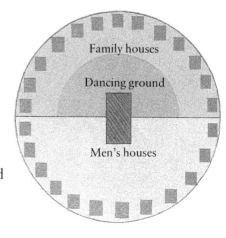

Family houses

Dancing ground

Men's houses

Living as a community *The entire village community of Yanomami lives under one roof. Eating, sleeping, fighting, talking, ceremonies, cooking, all take place in the "shibono" (above), reflecting the close relations among the people.*

Two halves of a whole *A traditional Bororo village (left) is divided in two; marriages can only take place between the two halves. Women own and run the family houses, but are forbidden in the men's house. The sacred heart of the community and the symbol of village unity is the dancing ground, used for rituals and ceremonies that bring all the families together.*

Children are thus less immediately tied to their parents and have a variety of role models and teachers. A child may have one blood mother, but also a number of secondary mothers. Among the Haida and Iroquois of North America, the maternal uncle takes care of a child (especially if male) after weaning. Each of the stages of life are marked by rituals, giving individuals a chance to assimilate their new identity and to acquire cultural experience. Each individual has a clear set of roles. The elderly are traditionally respected as "elders" and the ill cared for by the community.

Some social systems are designed to ensure order, stability, and cohesion. The Asmat in West Papua (Irian Jaya) offer substitute sons to their enemies and the Yanomami of Brazil and Venezuela exchange wives to re-establish peace after a conflict.

Even decisions about having a child are, in some societies, controlled by laws, helping to keep the population stable. In Melanesia children are adopted to rebalance the size of families.

The physical architecture of a village frequently reflects the social architecture of the people. Many forest-dwelling peoples, such as the Kayapo in Brazil, build their village around the men's house and the dancing ground – the centre of political and social life. In other communities, among the highlanders of West Papua (Irian Jaya), for instance, the chief's home is separated from the other houses to emphasize the social hierarchy. By contrast the Karen of Thailand, who have a high degree of household autonomy and social equality, have no village centre and all live in similar houses.

Social relations and identity run deep. Even when indigenous peoples are assimilated into mainstream society, social traditions remain intact. In West Papua (Irian Jaya), the Indonesian government considered the communal longhouses primitive and resettled highland people in rows of separate houses. But over time, the highlanders have added annexes until the houses join up and they can live much as before. For day-to-day interaction, closeness helps to reinforce a broader sense of community, though it may increase the risk of conflict. Although traditional economies, local forms of political authority, and even language have sometimes disappeared, among many peoples social relations persist as an important binding force.

Sharing spouses *In Tibet, before China invaded, it was traditional for men to have more than one wife and women more than one husband. This was often for economic reasons. Daughters were given away in marriage and sons inherited family land. If each son chose a partner, the land would be fragmented and the ancient family would disintegrate. So two or three brothers lived with one wife or several sisters would take the same husband. And the men did not ask who had fathered each child – the children simply called the eldest brother father and the others uncle. The institution of marriage was taken very seriously. Each union was arranged according to astrological predictions, as well as social status.*

BALANCING THE SEXES
The Quechua of the Andes

In most indigenous societies the roles of the sexes are clearly delineated and, if not always equal, are usually complementary. However, contact with "modern" society has, in many instances, weakened the position of women and broken down this traditional complementarity of roles.

In a Quechua village, land is controlled by both men and women, who inherit equally from their parents. Communities are divided into two groups – "upper" and "lower" – and marriage generally remains within the group. The aim of marriage is to join families and to combine land resources in the most advantageous way. Often there are several marriages between two families to bind further the two groups.

Women play a vital role in both income generation and household management. Men may periodically work on farms, but in many families the earnings are given to the women and administered by them.

Two factors have helped modify the traditional complementary relations between men and women. The first is the hacienda (large estate), which has created a situation of dependence. Generally only men are employed on them and often they must live there for part of the time. The women have to take on more responsibility for subsistence agriculture, while the men become active in the money economy. The balanced relationship of earnings is skewed in favour of men.

The second important change has been brought about by the Catholic Church. The Quechua worship the mountains and the Earth, and believe in an essential pairing of male and female principles. The Christian god, as a single, male god, is quite contrary to these beliefs.

Winnowing barley *A group of women and men work together in Caroa, Peru. Agricultural work is shared, although women often have the final say over the sorting and distribution of the harvest, and they may take on most of the herding activities. This means they earn their own money when eggs or milk are sold.*

THE AGE SET SYSTEM
The Maasai of East Africa

At the heart of Maasai culture is the "age set" system, which places those of the same age bands in groups. Strong friendships bind people for life. The system is both a continuous preparation for Maasai society and a means of giving each individual a place in the community.

From an early age, the duties of boys and girls differ. Girls remain with the female members of the household, collecting firewood, fetching water, milking cows and goats, and cooking. Boys tend the grazing animals, learning the basic skills of pastoralism from the elders, and move progressively away from the home.

At about the age of 16 both boys and girls are expected to possess the knowledge and experience to move to the next age set, and they are circumcized. Girls marry young elders and start a family. Boys are admitted to the warrior (*murran*) group when they have mastered the skills of rearing livestock, slaughtering animals, preparing food, setting up camp, and protecting against predators and thieves. Warriors defend the community and livestock, as well as ensure the wellbeing of their family herd. After about ten or twelve years as a warrior they undergo the *eunoto* ceremony, which tests their manhood, and they become tribal elders. Elders head the household and supervise husbandry, and they participate in public assemblies, where community matters are discussed exhaustively to achieve a consensus. Above all, elders try to harmonize the relations between age sets and between clans.

Oldoinyo le Engai *"The mountain of God" stands in the East African Great Rift Valley, near the Kenya-Tanzania border. It is an active volcano and the Maasai believe that its rumbling and flames indicate the presence of God, or Engai. The Maasai pray near it for children and cattle, and sacrifice pure white lambs.*

"Coward, the grey, colourless bird will be yours. Brave man, the red-winged touracos will be yours, and so will the green lovebirds." Song to a boy being circumcized

Circumcision *After puberty boys and girls are circumcized. On recovery boys hunt birds, which they attach to a headdress. If he has borne circumcision bravely a boy can collect colourful birds, but if he cried out he must collect dull-coloured ones.*

CHAINS OF ALLIANCE
The Kedang of Lembata, Indonesia

In many indigenous communities people are defined according to a basic criterion, such as whom they can or cannot marry. The effect is a conceptual pattern of marriage exchanges, or chains of alliance, which draws communities together into a web of interrelationships. These are reinforced with obligations and rights based on exchanges stretching from birth to death, connecting the living with the dead. One of the most vivid examples of how this works comes from the Kedang of Lembata.

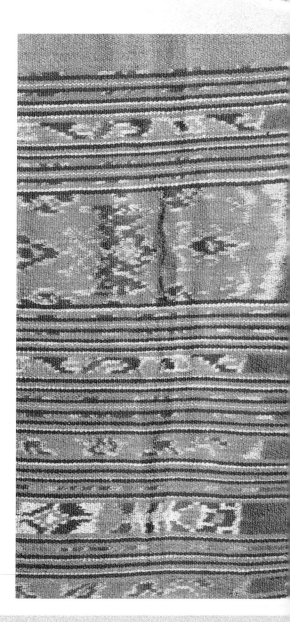

The Kedang community is made up of groups formed by a paternal descent line. Each descent group is related to the others by marriage, and the relationships between these groups bind together the whole social fabric. Each marriage establishes a wife-giving/wife-taking link, which is economic, political, and religious. Marriage must take place with a relative termed *mahan*, which includes a man's maternal uncle's daughter and a woman's paternal aunt's son. Wife-giving allies and, in particular, a man's or woman's mother's brother, play a major role in funerals, providing a special sarong called "steering the boat" and a piece of black cloth called "to show the way". Wife-givers receive a series of expensive gifts consisting of bronze gongs and elephant tusks, in stages, over a period that may extend beyond the lifetimes of the man and woman. In return, wife-takers receive finely woven, ikat cloths. Final confirmation that a marriage has been achieved comes with the last stage of gifts, often after the couple has died, and is carried out by children or grandchildren.

INDONESIA

Lembata

Marriage ikat *This* ikat adat, *a traditional, hand-woven fabric where the warp threads are tie-dyed prior to weaving, is one of several made by this Lembatan woman for her marriage 50 to 60 years ago. The cotton was grown in the hills and the rich colours come from natural dyes. The weaving alone took about three months and the whole process of spinning, dyeing, and weaving took about three years altogether. Patterns vary from village to village, and from one weaver to another.*

WAR AND PEACE

"Was it an awful war?"
"It was a terrible war."
"Were many people killed?"
"One man was killed."
"What did you do?"
*"We decided that those of us who had
done the killing should never meet
again because we were not fit to meet
one another."* San describing a war to
Laurens van der Post

Human beings are neither innately aggressive nor
peaceful. These are Western notions. The "peace-
loving" Inuit, Saami, or San have instances of
homicide and histories of warfare. And the
"warlike" Yanomami or Naga do not spend all
their waking hours raiding enemy villages and
ambushing victims. All peoples have ways of
avoiding violence and channelling it into socially
accepted forms. And each group uses the style that
fits with their world view and way of life.

The most common external cause of conflict is
scarcity of resources – land, crops, or marriageable
women. But for all warriors the personal aim in
fighting is to display their courage and skill, and so
receive status and prestige. Among the Dayaks of
Borneo, Igorots of the Philippines, and Nagas in
India, for example, men gain recognition and
admiration through becoming a warrior. Among
the Amazonian Shuar and Yanomami the most
able-bodied join a raiding party and the most
successful are treated as great hunters. Ambushing
the enemy is the most common form of raid,
although pitched battles did take place, among the
Dani of West Papua (Irian Jaya), the Bontoc in the
Philippines, and others.

Political alliances are a fundamental part of
fighting. According to one view enemies are fixed
and the hostility is on-going, so that "the enemy of
my enemy is my friend". Among other groups,
including the Nuer of East Africa, the enemy
depends on the size of the grievance. Those who
fight one day may well join to face a more powerful
enemy the next.

A warrior's life *The stereotype
of the Red Indian fails to present the reality of life for a
Plains warrior, nor his stature
among his people. The life
history of Sun Boy, a Kiowa
warrior from a noble clan
(right), depicts his raiding parties, ambushes, and battles
with Plains and Mexican
groups – a traditional part of
Indian life. Also shown are the
forced confrontations with the
cavalry, following colonization. Such autobiographical
stories were preserved by
Plains peoples as chronicles of
their history.*

Warfare is also about power. Many indigenous peoples see the individual as a receptacle of invisible power, connected to the energy that gives life its force. By capturing an enemy's power, a warrior can weaken him at the same time as increasing his own strength and power.

For those who prefer not to fight, competitive games provide an outlet for hostility between communities. Hockey among the Mapuche, polo in northern Pakistan, cricket and football in Melanesia and Amazonia all help to disperse aggression. Potlatch (see p. 43) on the west coast of North America may also be a way of channelling competition between chiefs.

Societies that value peace are found the world over. Among the Mbuti pygmies, only adult males with spiritual protection may show aggression. Northern peoples, such as the Saami and Inuit, have institutionalized ways of avoiding conflict and violence, often by shaming individuals who wish to impose their will on the group. In hunting and gathering cultures and those not based on hierarchies, conflict within the group and between groups is more easily controlled on an individual basis. The Piaroa of Venezuela, the Fipa of Tanzania, the Semai of Malaysia, and many others base their lives on co-operative exchange rather than competition to maintain a peaceful existence.

War and peace, however, are not mutually exclusive. Some peoples institutionalize both warlike and peaceful values. Each Cherokee town, for example, traditionally has a war chief and a peace chief. The White peace chiefs rule by consensus, while the Red war chiefs lead hunting and raiding parties. The situation determines who will lead. In many conflict situations, localized expressions of aggression may even help to ensure peace in the long term. For total warfare on the scale of the two World Wars – the destruction of land, resources, women, children and the old – is unknown among first peoples.

Six Nations Peace Belt *Political alliances formed between some groups rely on the peaceful resolution of differences. The Six Nations Iroquois Confederacy, or Haudenosaunee, for example, a union of the Mohawk, Oneida, Onondaga, Cayuga, Seneca, and Tuscarora nations, aims for harmonious accord. This is symbolized in the Six Nations Peace Belt (above). The six diamonds represent the lands and council fires of each nation. The unity of the Confederacy and its notions of freedom and justice were an inspiration to the settlers during the American War of Independence.*

INVISIBLE RULES
Maori justice

The Maori of Aotearoa (New Zealand) established a system of justice with a highly developed oratory, but no codified set of laws, courts, and judges. When the British imposed their own legal system on New Zealand, the rules took no account of Maori culture.

Traditional Maori justice was based both on the material and the spiritual worlds; redress for minor offences was determined by the community, more serious ones by the elders or chiefs.

Punishment would be exacted by a transfer of goods known as *utu*, or satisfaction, to the injured party. Persistent theft or murder, however, was punishable by *muru*, or plunder, but only after full and formal discussion with reference to the *ture*, or customary principles. Other offenders might receive a beating, the withdrawal of community assistance, or, worst of all, banishment.

In some respects there are similarities between traditional Maori law and that imported by the British. But the similarities ended with matters of the spirit world.

Chiefs with spiritual power could use it to conserve parts of the land for a feast. Access to the land was prohibited and violation would anger the spirits. Strangers unwittingly entering such areas would force the community to exact compensation, or even kill the intruder, in order to avoid being punished themselves by the spirits. Respect for the spirit world was fundamental to Maori society, but fell outside the comprehension of the British legal system.

Founding ancestors *Descended from deities, the founding ancestors gave their names to Maori tribes. This Maori meeting house on North Island contains a display of carvings depicting Maori ancestors. Here, a Tuhoe elder discusses the ancestors of the Tuhoe tribe with a young boy. The meeting house is the physical and spiritual locus of the tribe.*

WAR AS CULTURE
Papua New Guinea

World wars have torn societies apart, but not all societies are so destroyed by conflict. Within some indigenous communities, conflict is regulated by customary law. Rather than starting a war aggression is normally channelled into a ritualized process of war-making and long-term destruction is minimal.

In Papua New Guinea hostilities between groups are a part of the cycle of events encompassing long periods of peace and enmity. War is just one aspect of cultural life. The idea of annihilating the other group is absent; indeed, the Tsembaga and Mae Enga are known as the peoples who marry their enemies. War is a means by which the individual and the group find their identity, and is largely ceremonial.

War may be precipitated by theft, poaching, or – most serious – the killing of someone else's pig. Or long-standing enmities over territory and resources may create permanent hostilities. The Big Man, the non-hereditary chief, may try to avoid war by negotiating compensation or an exchange of gifts, but he cannot impose a decision. Equally, individuals do not take justice into their own hands as an unresolved dispute entails obligations for the whole group. But even on the point of war there is always a ritual means of stepping back from open confrontation. Anger can be channelled into a "nothing fight", a competition of insults and shouting. Or else it may lead to a real fight, with blows exchanged and sometimes even serious casualties. After a war a lengthy process of peace-making begins. Gifts, ceremonies, and marriages establish links and obligations between the parties.

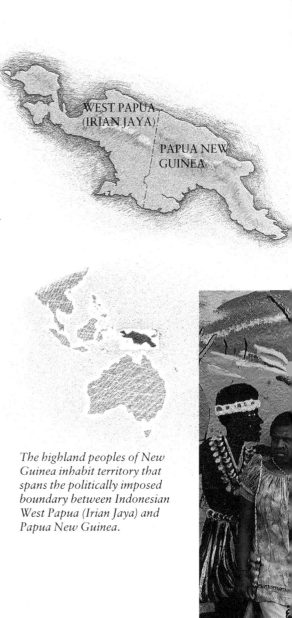

WEST PAPUA (IRIAN JAYA)

PAPUA NEW GUINEA

The highland peoples of New Guinea inhabit territory that spans the politically imposed boundary between Indonesian West Papua (Irian Jaya) and Papua New Guinea.

Living culture *Traditional styles of dance and dress are depicted in this Port Moresby mural.*

Challenge situation *Hostilities are generally governed by a code of conduct that determines the manner and means of fighting. However, in this instance (right), a challenge situation became serious and eventually had to be stopped by a third party.*

THE SPIRIT WORLD

"The Shaman knows that he is a spirit that seeks a greater Spirit. The great Spirit knows Death. Mother Earth knows Life. We were all born from the Spirit and once we have lived, we will return to the Spirit. The Shaman knows that Death is the Changer. We do not eat live food. We kill our animals. If the seed or berry does not die when it is plucked, it will die in the teeth or the caustic juices of the stomach. All Shamans know that Death furnishes all with Life."
Hyemeyhosts Storm, medicine man

First peoples see existence as a living blend of spirits, nature, and people. All are one, inseparable and interdependent – a holistic vision shared with mystics throughout the ages. The word for religion does not exist in many cultures, as it is so closely integrated into life itself.

For many indigenous peoples spirits permeate matter – they animate it. This led the early anthropologists to refer to such beliefs as "animist". Natural phenomena – hills, birds, animals, plants, trees, rivers – embody spirits. The Malaipantaram in southern India, for example, appeal to the spirits of the forested hills and rocky outcrops for protection, while in a trance.

There is often a close relationship between supernatural beliefs and social behaviour. Social events, especially moral transgressions, can trigger natural calamities. The Akawaio Indians of Guyana believe that disharmony within the community upsets the spirit world, giving rise to illness and misfortune. Acquisitiveness in some African traditions shows a lack of respect for the natural and spirit worlds and can cause sickness. Treating illnesses involves complex rituals – usually led by a shaman and involving the whole community – that aim to restore cosmic harmony. Funerals, too, draw the community together after a loss, while protecting it from potentially dangerous contact with the spirit world. In some societies, the spirit of

Tree spirit *Many indigenous cultures believe that spirits emanating from the natural world are incarnated in a human body for a lifetime and return to their source at death. When an Asante king dies, his shrine is laid on its side and returned to the wood of the tree, its spiritual origin (right).*

Modern spirit *For one group of Ayoreo Indians in Paraguay, a mining company has taken on the symbolic power of the enemy. Instead of a traditional jaguar or pig headband, several Ayoreo now wear a Castrol tin totem (below), hoping to appropriate the cunning the company displayed during a conflict over land in 1979.*

Demons of death *Spirits can threaten to snatch people away from life. The demon seen with his 18 servants on this Sri Lankan mask (below) can transmit fatal diseases over long distances. To rescue a victim from death, the shaman has to deceive the demon and negotiate with each servant.*

a person who died suddenly or accidentally remains at large and can threaten the community. Some Amazonian peoples eradicate the memory of the deceased so the spirit can merge with the invisible world. The Cree perform rituals for years after a death to ensure a good afterlife for the spirit. Approaches to death vary considerably, but many groups see birth and death as the transformation of life from one world to another.

The social and cosmic orders are reflections of each other. In North America, the four directions or winds incorporate all aspects of Indian life. Black Elk, an Oglala Sioux, describes the four ribbons on his pipe as the four quarters of the universe. *"The black one is for the west where the thunder beings live to send us rain. The white one for the north whence comes the great white cleansing wind; the red one for the east, whence springs the light, and where the morning star lives to give men wisdom; the yellow for the south, whence comes the summer, and the power to grow. But these four spirits are only one spirit, and the eagle feather here is for that one, which is like a father, and it is also for the thoughts of men that they should rise as high as the eagles do."*

Myths that explain the origins of the world remind people of their place in the universe and of their connection with the past. Some are humorously ironic, others complex and esoteric. Some, notably Aboriginal Dreamtime, speak of the creation of the hills, rocks, hollows, and rivers formed by powerful ancestral spirits in the distant past. Others describe a dramatic split between the gods and humankind or the severence of the heavens and the Earth – as in the sudden separation of the Sky Father and Earth Mother in Maori legend. Others tell the story of how the world was peopled, as in the sacred book of the Maya of Central America. Myths invest life with meaning. The rich symbolic associations found in the oral traditions of many indigenous cultures bring the sacred into everyday life – through a pipe, a feather, a rattle, a colour even – and help individuals to keep in touch with both themselves and the spirit world.

How the Sanema came to life
"Long, long ago the ancestors did not exist at all. A single ancestor there was only and that was Omao, the culture hero: and Omao was about to create the Sanema. Down by the big river Omao went to collect poli (hardwood trees with peeling bark). Having collected a single tree he went on downstream to find another. Returning with the single tree he came on his younger brother Soawe. 'Go and collect me more shidishina (Sanema)' Omao said to Soawe, and went off to collect more himself. 'Oh dear' said Soawe, 'my brother will expect me to collect this wood very quickly.' So he went out and hastily collected many lengths of kodalinase (softwood tree). When Omao returned he was angry. Omao made us Sanema from the kodalinase wood. 'I was going to make the Sanema from poli trees so that they could cast their old skins. Once they had become really elderly both husband and wife, they could have dived into the rivers and stripped off their old skins, and so become beautiful again,' Omao said. Because these weak trees had been collected the Sanema die really quickly. So we become weak. So we die. So we mourn, instead of being able to peel off our skins when we become really old, as we would like."

MUTUAL AID
Ritual offerings in Bolivia

Spanish conquerors in South America during the 16th century found austere and inhospitable surroundings in the high plains of Bolivia, yet the land supported one of the highest-density populations anywhere in the Americas. The Bolivian Indians work hard to produce sufficient food for the population. But they also harness the powers of nature to ensure fertility and good weather.

Night-time vigil *Aymara Indians make offerings to the deities of the sky, Earth, and underworld, who receive maize and blood sacrifices in rituals that last the whole night. Christian deities have also been worshipped since their introduction by the Spanish.*

There is a mutual relationship between the world of the spirits and their human worshippers. Offerings are made all through the year to the male mountains and the lightning – the lords of the weather and the flocks. The female Earth spirit, Pachamama, receives offerings during the cultivation season. Men and women pour libations of corn or barley beer and chew the sacred coca leaves to harness the powers of their universe.

Spirits and deities can be male or female, but all embody female and male elements. The Indians say "Everything is man and woman together". "Female" potatoes and "male" maize are the staple crops of the peasant economy.

The collective rituals and the spirits who animate the world provide focus for the hopes, labours, and anxieties of those who depend on the climate and soil.

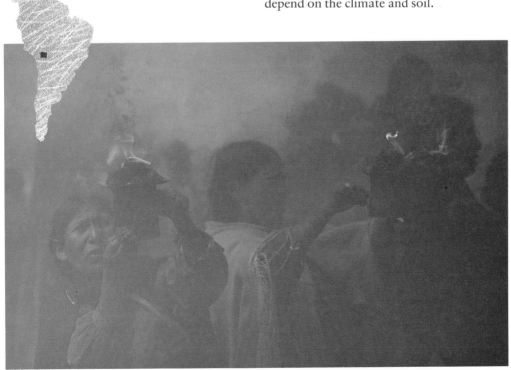

CHILDREN OF THE UNIVERSE
Creation for the Hopi Indians

The Hopi Indians of North America travelled far to reach their homeland. The Hopi creation story tells of their migrations and accounts for the wealth of their knowledge and prophecies about the rest of the world.

The first Hopi world was endless space. It took shape in the mind of Taiowa, the Creator. Taiowa created Sotuknang, who distributed the earth, water, and air. He also created Kokyangwuti, Spider Woman, who moulded the "first people". They came to life in three phases of colour – dark purple, yellow, and red. Each colour revealed, in turn, the mystery, the breath of life, and warmth of love. They were given different languages, respect for each other's difference, wisdom, and the power to reproduce and multiply. He asked them to respect the Creator, and to practise their gift of wisdom and harmony.

According to the legend, these "first peoples" understood themselves. They were happy and knew no sickness, multiplied and spread across the world. But when they forgot the commands of their maker, they began to argue and fight.

A few longed to live by the old laws and turned to Sotuknang for help. He told them to hide beneath the ground with the Ant People and be saved. Then he consumed the surface of the Earth with fire.

Sotuknang also brought an end to the second and third Hopi worlds. The "first peoples" crossed the seas in search of the Fourth World, the "World Complete". Finally they came to a land that was both hot and cold, abundant and barren, beautiful and ugly. Masaw, guardian spirit of the Fourth World, instructed them to travel in a series of migrations that would lead them to their home. The "first peoples" finally settled on the vast arid plateau between the Colorado River and the Rio Grande.

Petroglyphs *Carvings on the rocky outcrops portray the daily lives of the Hopi Indians. The vertical footprints, for example, indicate travel to the north or south. The style of the symbols can identify them with a particular clan. Several clans might occupy one village.*

Hopi villages *The oldest Hopi settlement still in existence is Old Oraibi, occupied since the 12th century. It and most of the other villages cling to escarpments of three rocky outcrops, or mesas, rising abruptly from the desert plains of northern Arizona and Utah.*

DREAMTIME
Ancestors and the Aborigines

Warramurrungundji came from the sea and created land. A female in human form, she gave birth to people and gave them their languages. Other creator beings were also given life: Ginga, the giant ancestral crocodile; Marrawuti, the sea eagle. The act of creation over, these ancestors put themselves into the landscape. Warramurrungundji is a white rock in the woodland; Ginga is a rock outcrop textured like a crocodile's back; Marrawuti brought waterlilies and planted them on the flood plain. These are "dream-sites", echoes of "dreamtime", and remain charged with the energy that created animals in their image.

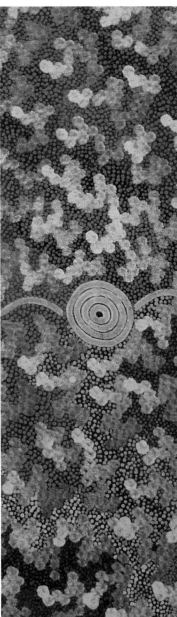

"Dreaming" and "dreamtime" are direct translations from Aboriginal words, but have little to do with dreams as we know them. Dreamtime refers to the beginnings of life more than 40,000 years ago; it is also the key to its continuation into the future. Human beings are instructed by the ancestors to maintain everything as it has been since Dreamtime.

The Aborigine culture developed when Aborigines formed co-operative tribal and family groups, setting up laws, expressing their daily lives through dance, creating artefacts, following the law, husbanding the resources of the land. They carried out communication by symbolized drawings, carvings, configurations on rocks, smoke fires, telepathy, inter-tribal symbols, initiation cycles, dance exchange, and complex language patterns. All are part of a refined civilization in existence long before written language was developed, a mere 5000 years ago.

Images of Dreamtime *The act of painting connects the artist with Dreamtime. Rock paintings 35,000 years old are thought to have been left behind by creator beings. The Aborigines continued the art using a mixture of clay and natural pigments. More common now is painting on strips of bark. The painting (below) shows the Kapi, or Water Dreaming, near Mount Wedge, South Australia. The concentric circles mark the place where two men of the Dreaming performed a rain-making ceremony.*

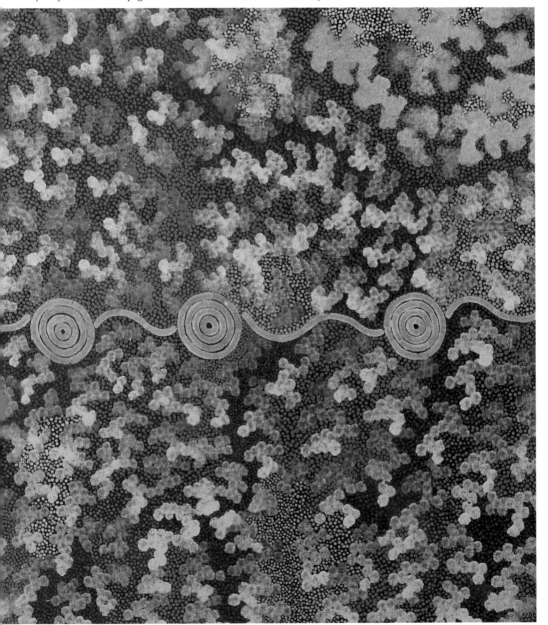

CHARGED WITH VITAL ENERGY
Shamanism in Colombia

The religious knowledge and practices used to explain the world and mediate between humankind and the creators vary enormously from one society to another. In many indigenous communities there is an intermediary – sometimes called a shaman – between the spirit and human world. The shaman tries to regulate relations to ensure harmony both within the community and between the community and the supernatural, or spirit, world.

The Ufaina, a Tukano-speaking people living in the northeastern part of the Colombian Amazon, believe that the world around them is charged with energy. Their daily life is influenced by this belief, and a shaman, known as the Jaguar Man, co-ordinates both practical wisdom and religious customs. He decides which rituals should be carried out and when the community should move to another place. He knows from experience which resources are in danger of being depleted, and he is guided by his spiritual foresight. His responsibilities include transferring spirit energy between the animal, human, and spirit world in order to prevent dangerous accumulation of invisible spirit substance and ensure the smooth flowing of life.

The Ufaina believe that there is a finite amount of energy. At birth some of this force enters the body; at death it returns to its source, from where it is recycled. This force is limited and must be controlled and carefully circulated through all living things. The Jaguar Man watches over individuals and the community to ensure that a harmonious balance is maintained between the different living domains.

Ceremonial dress *These headdresses, made of egret feathers, are used by the Makuna sub-group of the Tukano for ceremonial dances. They are considered very precious and are kept in a special woven cane box. The apron (foreground) is also worn at festivals.*

Other states of consciousness *Indians from the Barasana sub-group of the Tukano hand round a gourd of* chicha *during a festival. Chicha, coca, and certain hallucinogenic drugs are used as part of their rituals.*

PART TWO

CRISIS

Nothing has been so destructive to indigenous peoples as what we call progress. Mines, dams, roads, colonization schemes, plantations, cattle ranches and other expressions of "economic development" have forced indigenous peoples from lands they have occupied for centuries and severely damaged local environments. Deforestation, desertification and degradation of fragile, marginal lands first affect indigenous peoples, the traditional inhabitants. When they seek to stop a project, there are wider issues at stake. While certain development projects may bring real advantages to some, all too often benefits for the few are at the expense of the many. "Political progress" has also hit indigenous peoples hard. In the name of global security, their lands have been contaminated. They endure racism and oppression. And in most parts of the world they are colonized peoples, who have not voluntarily opted to become citizens of the nations of which they form a part. However, indigenous peoples do not believe they can return to some idyllic past of hunting and gathering, nor that they can remain isolated from the powerful political forces around them. They are opposed to a development which threatens their survival and the environments that regulate temperature and rainfall on a global scale, and keep the planet suitable for human habitation.

FIRST CONTACT

"In the long hundred years since the white man came, I have seen my freedom disappear like the salmon going mysteriously out to sea. The white man's strange customs which I could not understand, pressed down on me until I could no longer breathe. And when I fought to protect my land and home, I was called a 'savage'. When I neither understood nor welcomed the white man's way of life, I was called lazy. When I tried to lead my people, I was stripped of my authority." Chief Dan George, Vancouver

European colonialism has been one of the most destructive processes in human history. In 1492, the date of the arrival of Columbus in the Americas and the symbolic beginning of the tragic adventure, most of the world was unknown to the Europeans. Within 400 years, successive waves of expansion had pushed much of the world's original peoples off their lands and decimated their numbers.

The Europeans came bearing their civilization as if it were a gift. Yet to the people they deemed savage, whose well-ordered societies and rich cultures stretched back thousands of years, the gift was lethal. Contact with the outside brought not only murder and enslavement but disease and cultural disintegration. In Australia, a country designated by the white pioneers as "terra nullius" (or uninhabited), there were some 500 distinct peoples with different languages and well-defined territories. A century later, the population had been reduced to one-fifth.

The colonizers came with a sword in one hand and a Bible in the other, *"To bring light to those in darkness, and also to get rich"*, as the soldier-chronicler Bernal Diaz del Castillo put it. Impervious to the highly developed spiritual awareness of the people, they sought to convert them – often on pain of death – to an alien religion.

The Americas *In Central and South America, numbers of indigenous peoples fell from 30 to 5 million in 50 years. In North America, the population had dropped to 1 million by the 1890s; the Caribbean peoples were almost wiped out. Today, US Indians make up only 0.5% of the population. The bar chart (right) shows the decline of populations.*

North America
Central America
South America

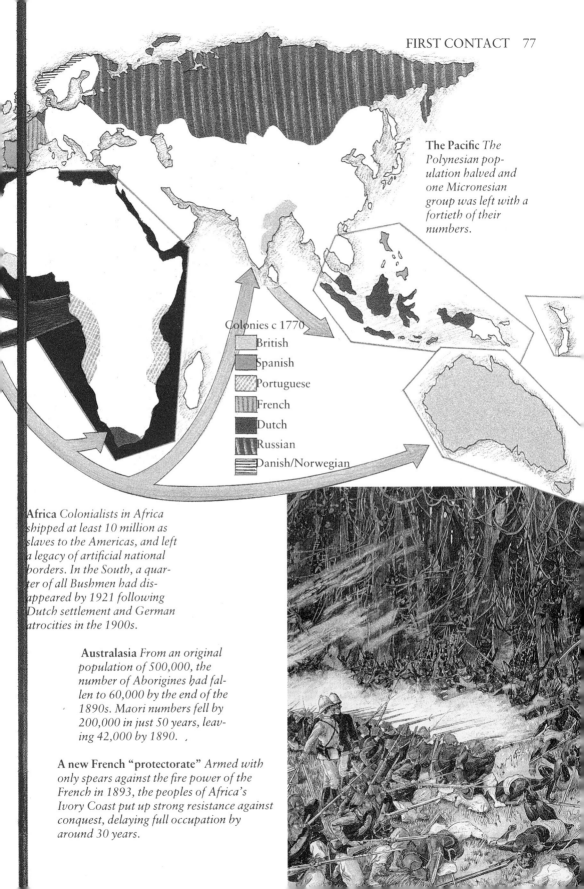

The Pacific *The Polynesian population halved and one Micronesian group was left with a fortieth of their numbers.*

Colonies c 1770

British
Spanish
Portuguese
French
Dutch
Russian
Danish/Norwegian

Africa *Colonialists in Africa shipped at least 10 million as slaves to the Americas, and left a legacy of artificial national borders. In the South, a quarter of all Bushmen had disappeared by 1921 following Dutch settlement and German atrocities in the 1900s.*

Australasia *From an original population of 500,000, the number of Aborigines had fallen to 60,000 by the end of the 1890s. Maori numbers fell by 200,000 in just 50 years, leaving 42,000 by 1890.*

A new French "protectorate" *Armed with only spears against the fire power of the French in 1893, the peoples of Africa's Ivory Coast put up strong resistance against conquest, delaying full occupation by around 30 years.*

MODERN COLONIALISM

"The white man's advanced technological capacity has occurred as a result of his lack of regard for the spiritual path and for the way of all living things. The white man's desire for material possessions and power has blinded him to the pain he has caused Mother Earth by his quest for what he calls natural resources."
Thomas Banyacya, Hopi village leader

Colonialism has not ceased, but continues with even greater intensity. The players, however, are different. Banks, corporations, speculators, governments, development agencies, and foreign power groups intervening by proxy are today's colonialists. Their actions are fueled by consumerism – a boom, led by the industrialized countries – and by the global population explosion. Demand for living space, food, consumer goods, and mightier military hardware has soared since World War II. Industrial production has grown by a factor of 40. Urbanization and industrialization, the twin symbols of modern life all over the world, have stimulated vast programmes of energy production in developing countries and the construction of over 100 superdams.
And superpower rivalry has brought even the most remote regions into the ambit of military strategists. Whether in the Arctic homeland of the Inuit or the Dreaming paths of the Aborigines of central Australia, military installations are now in place that will be key targets in the event of nuclear war. In the industrialized countries traditional indigenous lands have been used for bases and test sites; in developing countries their territories have sometimes become killing grounds.
   First peoples are in the frontline. They are sitting on resources the rest of the world wants, and wants at the lowest possible cost. Their territories are

Land of enchantment *The stereotyped view of indigenous peoples (depicted here by Creek-Potawatomi artist, Woodrow Crumbo), persists within modern colonialism. Attitudes of assumed superiority deny indigenous people their reality as human beings with basic rights.*

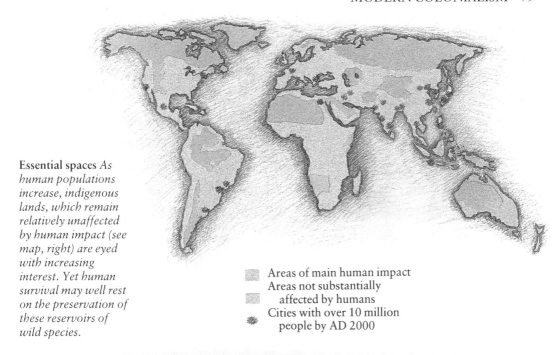

Essential spaces *As human populations increase, indigenous lands, which remain relatively unaffected by human impact (see map, right) are eyed with increasing interest. Yet human survival may well rest on the preservation of these reservoirs of wild species.*

Areas of main human impact
Areas not substantially affected by humans
Cities with over 10 million people by AD 2000

considered frontier lands, unowned,
underused and, therefore, open to
exploitation. More often than not their
populations are low in density, they are
politically weak and physically isolated. And, until
recently, their resistance has been relatively
ineffective.

The problem with economic growth

There is hardly a place in the world left untouched
by decisions taken in the boardrooms of New York,
London, Tokyo, or Frankfurt. And indigenous
peoples are increasingly at their mercy. Fluctuations
in commodity prices, the latest mergers, shifts in
exchange rates and trading terms – all can affect the
lives of indigenous peoples. A rise in oil prices
suddenly makes it profitable to invest in oil
extraction from Inuit lands in the Arctic. A slump in
demand for copper postpones a mining venture on
Guaymi territory in Panama.

Worldwide there are 50 large transnational
corporations each with annual turnovers higher
than those of one-third of the world's nation states.
Their capacity to invest with hard currency, to bring
in advanced technology and to create jobs lends
them formidable political influence. Poor countries
often offer them tax concessions and subsidies and
allow them to export both profits and resources.
Their presence has been felt throughout the world,
sometimes positive, but often negative – 200 sacred
sites desecrated in Aboriginal Australia; toxic
uranium tailings on Navajo land in the US.

Equally influential on development policy are the
multilateral development banks (MDBs). The four
largest – the World Bank, the Inter-American
Development Bank, the African Development Bank,
and the Asian Development Bank – together account
for 20 per cent of finance for development aid
projects. Furthermore, when MDBs participate in
the financing of a major project it serves as a
guarantee for hesitant investment by private banks
and companies. This promotes a Western model of
development since both private and public funds are
concentrated in the rich north. Although the World

*"We have elders alive now
who in their youth
supported up to 40 people
by hunting. Who of us with
our salaries today can
support ten?"*
Rene Lamothe, Inuit

Problems in developing world
o   Growing national debt
o   Poverty and overpopulation
o   Widening gulf between rich and p

National security threatened
o   Increase in forces of law and orde
o   Diversion of resources to arms
o   Reinforcement of economic mode

Involvement of rich countries
○ Loans from IMF amd World Bank
○ Investment by commercial banks and TNCs

Share of natural resources relative to world average

0.5 or less
0.6 or 1
1.1 to 3
Above 3

Hard-headed economy
Painted by a Mohawk high rise scaffolder, this hat depicts the fragmentation of *modern life, brought on by today's material culture – a development that threatens Mohawk lives and culture.*

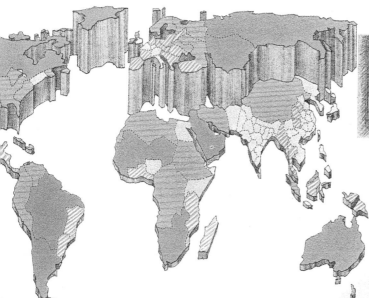

National development strategy
○ Opening up new lands
○ Incentives to foreign investors
○ Exploitation of resources
○ Production of crops for export

Traffic of wealth *Regions with a large share of natural resources are not necessarily those with a high gross national product (tall blocks on map). The mineral and land wealth often concentrated in marginal, indigenous lands flows into the financially rich industrialized First World. Brazil's GNP of $210 billion is equal to the assets of Credit Agricole, tenth down the list of top banks.*

Effect on indigenous people
○ Displacement
○ Impoverishment
○ Depletion of natural resources
○ Organization to defend land

Impact

Invasion
Development and military projects on indigenous lands trigger a crippling sequence of events. Indigenous peoples fight for survival. Some never recover.

Disease Measles, influenza, and sexually transmitted diseases, brought in by outsiders, are a common cause of death among indigenous peoples.

Violence First peoples try all legal means open to them to stop damaging projects. But governments have used guns to impose development.

Loss of home When their land is invaded, indigenous peoples are either forcibly removed or find they can no longer survive. Where new land is given it is rarely adequate.

Bank, for example, is controlled by all 151 participating countries, one-fifth of the voting rights are held by the USA, and more than half are in the hands of six major industrial countries.

Such development projects are often large-scale, dependent on high technology and sometimes damaging to the fragile habitats in which they take place. Proclaimed as being in the national interest, very often it is the First and Third World that are enriched, while the poor receive few of the benefits.

Bottom of the heap

The long-term effects of modern development projects on indigenous peoples are all too often catastrophic. Once divorced from their lands, their independent way of life, and group support, they seek survival within the dominant, national society. Yet when they do, it is usually at the lowest level. Only 4 per cent of Maoris have professional jobs; more than half the Ainu in Japan are believed to be illiterate; the number of Australian Aborigines out of work is five times the national average. The income of native Americans in the USA is half the national average, and the majority of India's tribal people live below the poverty line. The life expectancy of the indigenous peoples of northern USSR is 18 years less than the average for the whole country. Indigenous peoples are offered the least schooling, medical care and welfare, the worst housing, and the lowest salaries.

Move to towns Without land and livelihood they are forced to make their homes in squatter camps (see above) or town slums, where conditions are poor and unhealthy. Often they are forced to live on social welfare or travel hundreds of miles in search of work.

Discrimination Since they have few of the accepted qualifications, indigenous peoples are considered unsuitable for employment. And many suffer discrimination from bosses who consider them lazy.

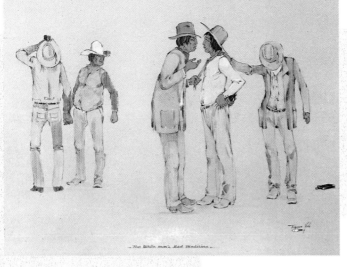

Trapped in transition In *White Man's Bad Medicine* (left), Creek-Seminole, Jerome Tiger depicts the indigenous trap. Proud warriors, deprived of a role in white society, drink to hold on to their masculinity, only to fall prey to the stereotype of the drunken Indian.

Loss of personal identity When people lose their cultural identity and are cut off from their spiritual roots in the land, they lose the meaning of their lives, their self-esteem, and their sense of belonging. They are left with a profound sense of demoralization. Frustration can lead to alcohol and drug abuse; despair can end in suicide.

Loss of cultural identity Without land and economic independence traditional values break down and customs and group ties splinter. This brings loss of dignity, of language, of respect for elders, and a sense of disorientation.

Crime and prostitution In order to survive, some turn to petty crime or prostitution. Others are vulnerable to exploitation or depend on food handouts.

The prejudices that characterized the colonial era persist in neo-colonialism. In isolated regions indigenous peoples risk being abused, exploited, and enslaved. A 1978 report to the United Nations revealed that Ache Indians in Paraguay were being captured and sold for five dollars each to landowners, for clearing land under the supervision of military units. A 1984 investigation found that up to 90 per cent of Yagua Indians in northeast Peru were caught up in a patron system that left them wholly dependent on local landowners and employers. In Asia, many millions of indigenous peoples are literally enslaved by debt bondage. India, for example, has 5 million bonded labourers, most of them indigenous and many born into bondage because their fathers borrowed a few rupees.

There are notable exceptions. A Maori, Paul Reeves, is Governor-General of New Zealand. Xavante Indian, Mario Juruna was federal deputy for Rio de Janeiro from 1983 to 1986. Members of scheduled tribes in India have reached ministerial positions. And Maori opera singer Kiri Te Kanawa and Aboriginal actor David Gulpilil are well-known international figures. These successes give inspiration, but they belie the overwhelming discrimination that blocks the path of those indigenous peoples who try to fulfil their potential – and even to survive – within modern society.

INVASIONS

"Too many people bring suffering to the land, and the land returns its suffering to the people."
Dr O Soemarwoto, Institute of Ecology, Bandung, Indonesia

First peoples' homelands are also targets of internal colonialism, and even of outright military occupation. They often inhabit lands in deserts, forests, tundra, or mountain regions – environments that cannot support large populations in the long term. Yet governments view these lands as areas that might absorb growing numbers.

Large-scale development projects, declining terms of trade and poverty have sent governments in the developing countries in search of foreign assistance. Since then, interest rates on the loans have created crippling debts and increasing dependence on the rich nations. The national development strategies elaborated by the ruling élites of these poor countries, as well as the governments, banks, corporations, and other investors in the First World, are largely based on the intensive exploitation of the country's natural resources in order to generate foreign exchange through exports to pay off loans.

The growth of agribusiness – large-scale commercial agriculture – has caused widespread landlessness and forced many peasants to farm the fragile soils of hillsides and forests. Governments, notably in Brazil, Peru, Bangladesh, Indonesia, and the Philippines, have promoted resettlement programmes, moving "surplus people" to marginal areas, frequently on indigenous lands.

Increasing populations and poverty have also brought political instability. Although 80 per cent of military expenditure is accounted for by NATO and the Warsaw Pact, spending on arms in the developing world doubled between 1978 and 1988. In these countries, where indigenous peoples are concentrated, there are currently nearly 60 military regimes and over 20 major conflicts.

White curiosities *A humorous Balinese depiction of the invasion of Westerners into traditional rural life.*

Pressure on the land *The world's population rises by 1 million every four days, most rapidly in areas close to indigenous lands (see map, right). Numbers in India, Africa, Southeast Asia, Latin America, and the Middle East are increasing three times as fast as the rest of the world, bringing ever-greater numbers on to the fragile lands of first peoples.*

800 billion

From birth to bombs *The UN estimates that the global population will rise to 10 billion before stabilizing. As pressure on resources has spiralled, so has political instability. Military spending in developing countries has more than doubled in a decade. The graph (below) shows the link.*

US$200 billion

1 billion people

World War II

AD 900   Population increase

AD 2025

1925   Military spending   1975

CONQUEST BY NUMBERS
Transmigration in Indonesia

Indonesia, with the fifth-largest population in the world – 170 million – has embarked on a programme that aims to move millions of landless villagers from the densely populated central islands of Java, Madura, and Bali to the sparsely populated outer islands of Kalimantan, Sulawesi, Sumatra, and West Papua (Irian Jaya). Over 60 per cent of Indonesia's population lives on the central islands, which make up only 7 per cent of the total land area.

Transmigration is based on two main assumptions. The first is that over-population can only be resolved by exporting surplus people. The second is that the outer islands are underdeveloped and need new inhabitants and cash crops.

Opinions on the value of transmigration vary widely, but one fact is conclusive: intensive crop cultivation on cleared land is causing irrevocable destruction of the forests on which local people depend. Rain forest loss is estimated at 1 million hectares a year, with transmigration exacting a large part of that toll.

For the indigenous peoples transmigration is a major catastrophe. Their lands are seized with little or no compensation and they face racial discrimination and forced assimilation to bolster "national unity" through "ethnic integration".

Up to 1986 the World Bank had contributed over half a billion dollars and agreed in 1988 to provide US$150 million more. To the Bank it is an investment in national development, but to indigenous peoples it is a policy to oppress them in their own lands, condoned and supported by the West.

Migrations *By the end of Indonesia's fifth five-year plan, 10 million people will have been resettled. During the first three plans (1969-84) more than 3.5 million were moved. In the fourth five-year plan, 3.8 million. The present plan (1989-94) will see about 2.7 million people relocated.*

Sumatra

10 million people resettled		
3.5 mill.	3.8 mill.	2.7 mill.
1969-84	84-89	89-94

Over-population *Around 60 per cent of Indonesia's 170 million people currently live on 7 per cent of the archipelago's land area – on Java and Madura. On Java there are approximately 700 people per square kilometre, and the population increases by 2 million every year. At best, only 25 per cent of this increase is absorbed by resettlement. By contrast West Papua (Irian Jaya), the target of transmigration over the next decade, has a population of 3 people per square kilometre.*

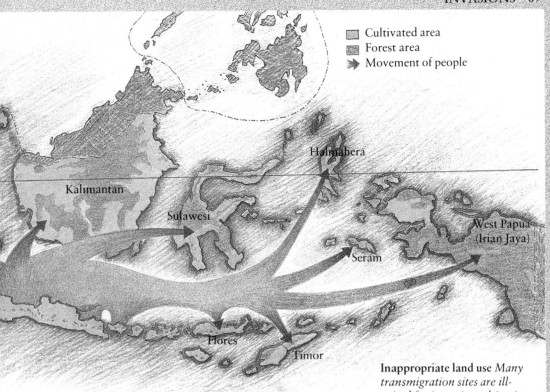

Cultivated area
Forest area
Movement of people

Halmahera

Kalimantan

Sulawesi

Seram

West Papua
(Irian Jaya)

Flores

Timor

Inappropriate land use *Many transmigration sites are ill-suited for intensive cultivation; the soils are not fertile enough to sustain more than a few successful harvests. In Kalimantan, for example, less than 2 per cent of the soils are thought to be permanently cultivable. The indigenous peoples have been able to survive precisely because they have evolved methods of cultivation suitable for poor soils. Indigenous agro-forestry allows the land to lie fallow and regenerate, and fully makes use of other food sources. This method is considered primitive and backward by the Indonesian authorities, who are promoting commercial agriculture.*

DEFORESTATION

"We are fighting to defend the forest. It is because the forest is what makes us, and what makes our hearts go. Because without the forest we won't be able to breathe and our hearts will stop and we will die." Paulinho Paiakan, Kayapo leader

Shrinking forests *By the year 2000, virtually all primary forest in Guatemala, India, the Philippines, Malaysia, and Thailand will have gone. About 7-8 million indigenous people will lose their forest home. The map (above) shows the current area of rainforest.*

Today, the world's rainforests are home and a source of life to 50 million indigenous people. The relationship is mutually supportive and allows both to thrive. The forest provides food, clothing, medicines, and shelter. It is a familiar place full of spirits that teach, protect, warn, and nourish. In return, the people use their profound knowledge to care for the trees, plants, and other animals. They fish, hunt, and gather without depleting resources and cultivate a wide range of crops without damaging the environment.

Deforestation alienates forest people from themselves and each other. It brings disease, conflict, displacement, sometimes death. Most vulnerable are those who have previously had little contact with outsiders. Among some groups of Venezuelan Yanomami, for example, measles and whooping cough brought in by outside workers have wiped out more than 30 per cent of the population. In Sarawak, where one-third of the forest has been felled in the last 30 years, only 450 Penan out of a population of 10,000 continue to live from the forest. The rest are settled in villages and towns.

Governments in the world's major forest zones see the rainforests as treasure chests that will pay off colossal foreign debts and fuel the leap into the 21st century. Consumer demand in industrialized countries for wood, beef, and forest products – together with huge foreign investments to extract minerals – appear to promise an answer. In Central America, the profitable US market for beefburgers stimulated 40 per cent of forest clearance to make

Soils in Sumatra are unable to recover following deforestation.

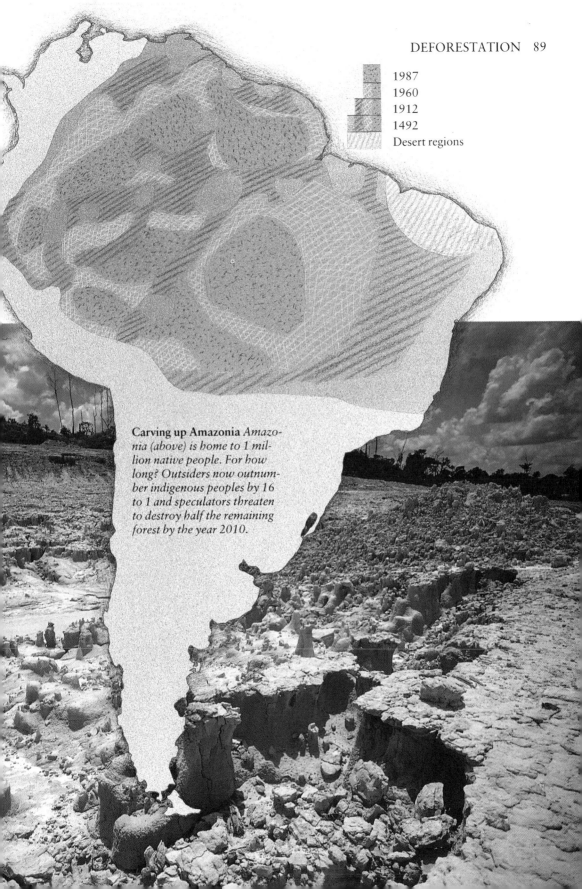

1987
1960
1912
1492
Desert regions

Carving up Amazonia *Amazonia (above) is home to 1 million native people. For how long? Outsiders now outnumber indigenous peoples by 16 to 1 and speculators threaten to destroy half the remaining forest by the year 2010.*

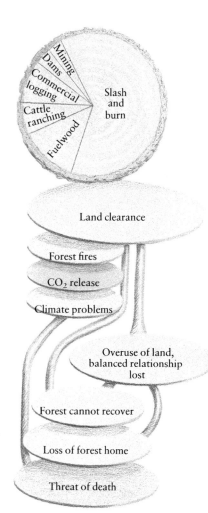

way for cattle ranches. Demand for hardwoods has stimulated commercial logging throughout Asia. In Japan, tropical timber imports have increased almost 20 times since 1950 and are still rising.

Population pressure forces millions of poor people to clear forest land for farming. But migrant farmers, cattle ranchers, loggers, and prospectors lack a true understanding of the forest. Plagued with plant diseases, weeds, and declining soil fertility, they are forced to clear new areas of forest. They slash and burn, but give the land no time to regenerate. The soil erodes and lowland areas flood, giving the forest little chance of recovery. And indigenous people who would protect the forest are pushed out. As wood becomes scarce, people are forced to collect firewood that would otherwise break down and enrich the soil. In addition forest fires release carbon dioxide into the atmosphere. This has already brought droughts and floods and threatens more serious, permanent climate changes (see pp. 120-1).

Cutting down trees solves neither economic nor social problems – even in the short term. Instead it creates new, potentially catastrophic, human and environmental crises. Some countries have tried to mitigate the problem by planting trees. But when primary forests are replaced with a monoculture of commercial timber, there is little fuel and no forest produce for the local people. Yet indigenous people maintain an open mind. *"We are not opposed to others living and benefiting from the jungle, nor are we opposed to its development. On the contrary, what we want is that this development should benefit us, and not just the companies and colonists from outside. And we want the resources of the jungle to be conserved so that they can serve future generations of both colonists and Indians."* Amarakaeri Indian, Peru. Unless we radically alter our policies, there will be no significant areas of tropical forest left for future generations.

An unsustainable situation
When forest is cleared for settlement, agriculture, grazing, mining, dams, logging, or to supply fuel, there are three interrelated repercussions. Indigenous peoples lose their land and their role as forest managers; the land is overexploited and given little chance to recover; and uncontrolled forest fires release carbon dioxide, causing the "greenhouse effect" and adding to climate problems.

COLONIZING THE FOREST
The Polonoroeste development, Amazonia

The quest for timber and land in rain forest areas necessitates the construction of roads that open the door to widespread colonization. The result is the destruction of forest and the establishment of short-lived cattle ranching on indigenous land.

In the west central region of Brazil the Polonoroeste development programme is a road-building and colonization project affecting about 10,000 indigenous people. The backbone of the scheme is the BR-364, linking Cuiaba with Rio Velho in Rondonia. In 1981 the World Bank approved a loan of $300 million. They describe the project area as *"an important agricultural and timber-producing region of Brazil and a place where migrants . . . may be productively and permanently settled . . ."*. In fact, the area is totally unsuitable for large-scale settlement. Less than 10 per cent of the soil is appropriate for intensive agriculture, according to the World Bank's own study, but much of the land is occupied by indigenous peoples. According to some critics the Bank's investment has *"contributed to uncontrolled migration, accelerated deforestation, conversion of land to unsustainable cattle-ranching, land speculation, and increased encroachment on Indian areas"*. The Bank abandoned funding in 1986.

Landsat images *In 1973 the road was a single track (below left). By 1987 an intense grid of roads had spread across the area (below).*

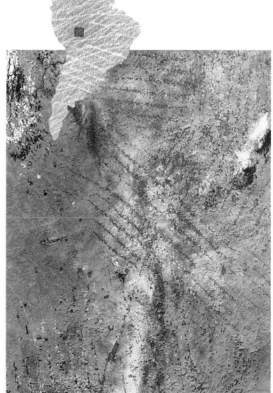

ECONOMIC OCCUPATION
Palm oil in Ecuador

Quichua
1 A'l
2 Siona-Secoya
3 Huao
Waorani forest
Waorani territory
Yasuni National Park
— Existing road
-- Proposed road
Oil concession
Palm oil plantation
Approximate extent of "conservation zone"

Over the last 30 years governments have earmarked Amazonia for economic expansion. Oil and plantation companies, ranchers and poor colonists are flooding into the area. In Ecuador some 60,000 Amazonian people are currently losing their land. In Ecuador 900 Waorani stand to lose the last of their forests to oil companies, and 35,000 Quichua people are threatened by palm oil plantations.

Today's threat to Ecuador's Indians is petroleum, tomorrow it could be palm oil. Nine oil consortiums have been granted concessions on Waorani land. In 1983 the Waorani were given title to 67,000 hectares – a fraction of their original territory. And this entire area, plus a 250,000-hectare forest reserve set aside for their use, is now open to the petroleum industry. An access road already penetrates the reserve, bringing hundreds of illegal settlers.

Oil production currently accounts for 70 per cent of Ecuador's exports. But over the next ten years palm oil is due to become Ecuador's principal money earner. Considerably more forest is lost for palm oil plantations than for petroleum extraction. The 20,000 hectares already planted with African palm are due to be expanded to 200,000 hectares. And according to CONFENIAE, the alliance of indigenous organizations in Ecuador's Amazon, about 35,000 Quichua people will be affected. Several communities have already had to stop fishing because pesticides used by one plantation company have contaminated the River Huashito.

The Amazonian lowland forest in the northeast of Ecuador is homeland to over 60,000 indigenous people. In the last 20 years 15% of forest has been destroyed by oil production, which depends on foreign investment. The nine major oil companies on Waorani land include BP, Conoco, Elf, Esso, Braspetro, and Petro Canada.

Crossed spears *This sign is cut into tree bark by the Waorani as warning to keep out. They have rejected deals with oil companies and clashed violently with missionaries and illegal settlers invading their forests. One in every six Indians has died following contact with outsiders.*

PERU

ECUADOR

Tomorrow's Waoranis *This Waorani girl's future depends on the activities of oil companies. Working on her side is CONFENIAE, an indigenous organization pushing the government for land rights and sustainable forest development. Neither petroleum nor palm oil has brought benefits to indigenous people. After initially using a few indigenous labourers for forest clearance, the major oil companies and plantations now employ only whites and mestizos.*

TREES, THE NEW GOLD
Logging in Sarawak

Trees now represent a new currency in many developing countries. In Malaysia, timber is a major export earner, fetching around US $1.4 billion in 1989. The export trade is dominated by foreign, mainly Japanese, interests and almost all the concessions are owned by politicians, their relatives, or their companies. It is the indigenous inhabitants who lose the most.

In March 1989 the Penan set up guarded barricades across roads deep in Sarawak's tropical forest. This was part of their growing campaign to stop the logging companies devastating the forest on a massive scale. So far over 300 arrests have been made and all protestors risk prison sentences of two years and fines of M $6,000. But the resistance has not stopped.

Malaysia contains the world's oldest forests, dating back 150 million years. But 700,000 hectares of it are logged every year – three hectares a minute. Between 1963 and 1985 2.8 million hectares – 30 per cent – of Sarawak's forests were felled and 5.8 million more hectares licensed out as logging concessions. At this rate of felling, all natural forest, except small areas of national park, will have disappeared in the next two decades.

As the trees come down, erosion damages the soils, water supplies become polluted, food sources disappear, and introduced diseases bring sickness. Those Dayaks who have settled in the towns have often faced low standards of living, but survive because, in the words of a Penan leader: "the land is always there to give us what we need." But this is now in jeopardy.

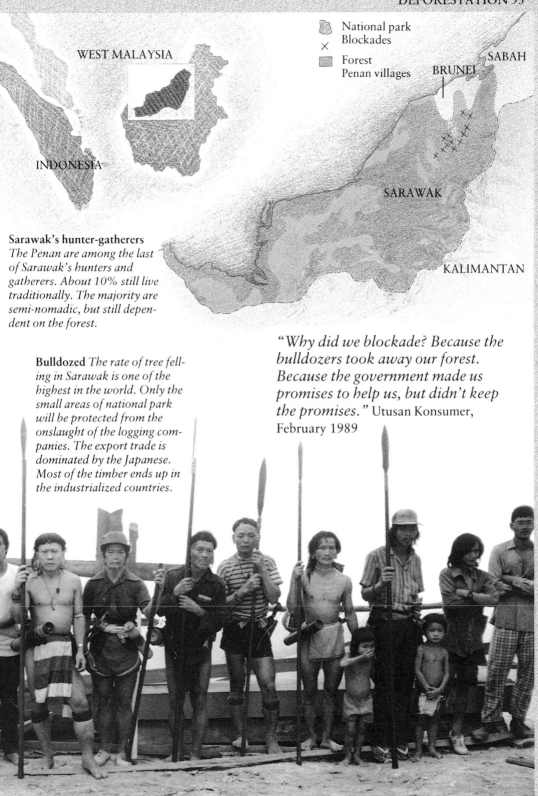

National park
× Blockades
Forest
Penan villages

WEST MALAYSIA

INDONESIA

BRUNEI

SABAH

SARAWAK

KALIMANTAN

Sarawak's hunter-gatherers
The Penan are among the last of Sarawak's hunters and gatherers. About 10% still live traditionally. The majority are semi-nomadic, but still dependent on the forest.

Bulldozed *The rate of tree felling in Sarawak is one of the highest in the world. Only the small areas of national park will be protected from the onslaught of the logging companies. The export trade is dominated by the Japanese. Most of the timber ends up in the industrialized countries.*

"Why did we blockade? Because the bulldozers took away our forest. Because the government made us promises to help us, but didn't keep the promises." Utusan Konsumer, February 1989

DAMMING

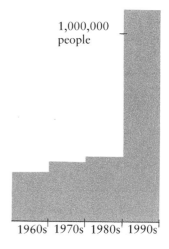

"This land is where we belong — it is God's gift to us and has made us as we are . . . If we had to move, we would be lost to those who remain in the other villages. This would be a sadness to us all, like the sadness of death. Those who moved would be strangers to the people and spirits and places where they are made to go."
The Akawaio Indians, Guyana, 1977

By the end of the decade there will be well over 100 superdams, 49 of them built during the 1980s. In developing countries — where hydropower now accounts for more than 40 per cent of electricity — dams can appear to be the key to economic development. They provide a renewable energy source for cities and industry, based on natural resources and apparently less damaging technology than nuclear and fossil-fuel power stations. And their spin-offs include an assured fresh water supply and improved irrigation.

But for indigenous peoples the costs can be devastating. Dams displace thousands, sometimes hundreds of thousands of people, flooding sacred sites, destroying homes, and inundating fertile soils and forests. Some 100,000 Chakma in Bangladesh were removed from their lands to make way for the Karnaphuli reservoir. The Tucurui and Itaipu dams in Brazil have together forced 50,000 forest dwellers from their land. And over 3 million may be forcibly resettled in China.

Dams also have wider costs, to be weighed against the benefits. They reduce the flow of rich silt downstream, leaving large low-lying areas infertile. They create reservoirs where vegetation rots and emits poisonous hydrogen sulphides. They disrupt aquatic ecosystems, causing a decline in river flora and fauna populations. They block seasonal fish migrations upstream. And they leave artificial stagnant lakes that often become breeding grounds for diseases such as malaria and bilharzia (snail

● Dams affecting indigenous peoples
  Completed/under construction
  Proposed
● Shelved/cancelled

Approaching a watershed?
Over 1 million mainly indigenous people could be affected if proposed or currently shelved dams go ahead (see map, above). Brazil, Chile, Costa Rica, India, Malaysia, and the Philippines are countries to watch. Around 350,000 people have been affected by hydro-electric projects in the 1980s (see graph below), more than 220,000 in the Philippines alone.

1,000,000 people —

1960s 1970s 1980s 1990s

Tribal people bathing downstream of the Bargi Dam in Narmada, India.

fever). New roads force more land clearance, and incoming construction workers bring imported diseases and social disruption.

Indigenous people are frequently not even informed of plans the authorities have for their land. The first knowledge local people had of the Kutku dam in Bihar, India, was when huts were constructed for the workers and surveyors began to walk across their fields with tape measures and levels. Nor are they generally compensated for their losses (see p. 99).

Moreover, dams often end by benefiting one small sector of the population – usually industry and city dwellers many miles away – at the expense of those in the majority locally. And although they promise cheap power for development, superdams are not proving so cost effective in the long term. Few dams last their expected life as reservoirs silt up and turbines are blocked by vegetation. Large funds are needed to counteract unforeseen flooding, salinization, and dam failure. In India, almost one-quarter of the land under irrigation has been devastated by waterlogging and salt.

Understanding and thoughtful planning are crucial when initiating a dam. The costs, the scale of the dam and the question of who benefits need careful consideration. Increasingly, the voice of indigenous people is getting through (see pp. 164-5). But for each success there are many losses. *"This land was given to us by our ancestors and we have every right to the land. This also applies to the river. I would like my children to know that the river is part of our life. What will happen to us when the clever men close the river?"* Purari Pastor, Papua New Guinea

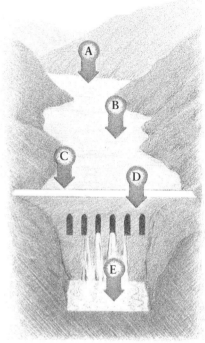

Damming the environment
Dams, particularly superdams, can change the whole ecology of a region. Natural resources disappear under water, including hunting and agricultural lands, while landslides into the reservoir can cause tidal waves and further overflow (A). The water in the reservoir can be poisoned by hydrogen sulphides emitted from decomposing vegetation and dioxin-based defoliants used to destroy the vegetation (B). Silt building up behind the dam blocks the movement of fish and shortens the life of the dam (C). Since the technology of large dams is still in its infancy, the danger of collapse remains (D), while extra salinity and reduced silt depletes the soils downstream (E). The dam, the infrastructure, and the colonists leave the indigenous population with little land.

WHAT COMPENSATION?
Damming the Narmada River

Hydroelectric power and schemes for irrigation promise an economic miracle for the poor western states of India. But can the government calculate the damage to the environment or to the displaced peoples for purposes of compensation?

The plan to irrigate several million hectares of land around the Narmada River and provide electricity to the poorer states of western India was supported by the World Bank in 1985.

The scheme is one of the largest in Indian history, and will cost US$19 billion over 25 years. But its side effects will include the inundation of agricultural land, religious and historic sites, and the displacement of up to 1 million, mostly tribal, people.

The World Bank was criticized for supporting the scheme without completing studies of its social and environmental impact, and not ensuring that resettlement land was being offered, or that proposed compensation plans were adequate.

The first major dam, at Sardar Sarovar, would alone displace 80,000 people, a largely tribal population of Bhils, Bhilalas, Vasaras, Tadaris, and Ratras. As many as 289 villages will be flooded as will over 10,000 hectares of forest and agricultural land used for wheat and cotton. Even the derisory compensation offered is unlikely to materialize and land for resettlement is virtually non-existent. Mortality rates in the few resettlement villages are high.

The question of compensation is part of a broader concern: can the economic gains ever outweigh the human and environmental chaos that will result?

The Narmada River, 1300km (800 miles) long, runs from east to west across most of the Indian subcontinent.

Environmental chaos *Living by one of more than 3000 dams and barrages planned for the Narmada River does not ensure compensation. Loss of woodland and waters used for hunting and fishing is not paid for and smallholdings, crops, and fruit-bearing trees are frequently undervalued. Resettlement often means being dispersed to distant villages, where mortality rates are high.*

BROKEN TREATIES
Canadian Cree resist dam

The Cree Indians fought and won their battle with the provincial government of Quebec to reach agreement before starting work on a large hydroelectricity project on their land. The James Bay and Northern Quebec Agreement was signed in 1975, but the government still attempts to construct dams and barrages before obtaining the agreement of the Cree.

The Cree Indians occupy the hinterland of James Bay, Canada. Traditional hunters, fishermen, and trappers, the Cree had no regional leadership when they first heard about the plans for the hydroelectricity project. Their rights were formalized only after a long battle (see right).

The James Bay and Northern Quebec Agreement has given the Cree exclusive hunting, fishing, and trapping rights in some areas of their territory, local self-government, and cash compensation.

In addition, the consent of the Cree is now required for all future development. In return, however, the Cree have had to surrender their aboriginal title to about 1 million sq km (400,000 sq miles) of northern Quebec. Despite a projected revenue of $1 billion a year, the cash compensation is meagre, and some of the funding has still not yet been approved.

Since the agreement was signed, a second phase of the project has been launched, without consultation. In 1989 the Cree began new litigation based on their right to consultation and the need for their consent for all future development. Such consent has not been given.

Environmental impact *Organic mercury is poisoning fish in the flooded Cree hunting lands. It is produced from inorganic mercury by the action of bacteria on the peat, or muskeg, on the shores of the reservoirs. The government has cautioned people not to eat the fish. This, and the deforestation by logging companies taking advantage of the dam-construction roads, have hit at the heart of traditional Cree life. Some Cree will receive no electricity from the scheme.*

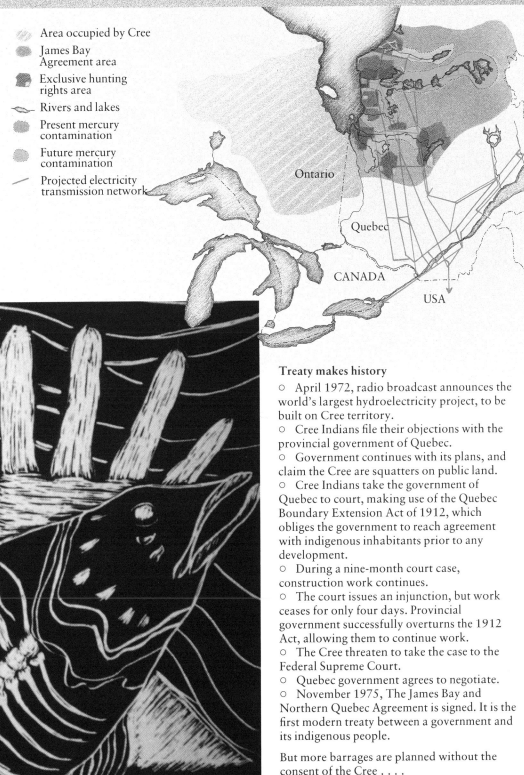

Area occupied by Cree

James Bay
Agreement area

Exclusive hunting
rights area

Rivers and lakes

Present mercury
contamination

Future mercury
contamination

Projected electricity
transmission network

Ontario

Quebec

CANADA

USA

Treaty makes history

○ April 1972, radio broadcast announces the world's largest hydroelectricity project, to be built on Cree territory.

○ Cree Indians file their objections with the provincial government of Quebec.

○ Government continues with its plans, and claim the Cree are squatters on public land.

○ Cree Indians take the government of Quebec to court, making use of the Quebec Boundary Extension Act of 1912, which obliges the government to reach agreement with indigenous inhabitants prior to any development.

○ During a nine-month court case, construction work continues.

○ The court issues an injunction, but work ceases for only four days. Provincial government successfully overturns the 1912 Act, allowing them to continue work.

○ The Cree threaten to take the case to the Federal Supreme Court.

○ Quebec government agrees to negotiate.

○ November 1975, The James Bay and Northern Quebec Agreement is signed. It is the first modern treaty between a government and its indigenous people.

But more barrages are planned without the consent of the Cree . . . .

MINING

"These people have already made the place no good with their bulldozers. Our sacred places they have made no good. They mess up our land. They expose our sacred objects. This breaks our spirit. We hate ourselves as people. What will we as a people do if these people continue to make all our land no good? Today we beg you that you truly stop them." The Yungngora community, Australia

Mining activity has escalated in the last 30 years to satisfy the demand for energy, consumer goods, and military technology. And as older, lower-grade reserves become too expensive to work, mining companies eat further into tropical forests, mountain sides, deserts, tundra, and coastal areas – traditional indigenous lands.

In Australia, nearly all significant mineral reserves are on Aboriginal land. In the USA, the Department of Energy estimates that between 25 and 50 per cent of uranium, one-third of all strippable coal and 2 per cent of oil and natural gas are on Indian reserves. One of the largest undeveloped coal mines in the world is on Guajiro land in Colombia, South America. Asia's biggest iron ore mine and one of India's largest foreign exchange earners is at Bailadilla, near Bastar in the heart of the Dandami people's lands. The second most important source of nickel outside the USSR is on Kanaky territory on the South Pacific island of New Caledonia.

Mining is the greatest single threat to indigenous people. It pollutes vital water supplies, it imposes a debilitating economy and alien social values, it destroys sacred sites, disfigures familiar landscapes, and separates people from their homes, their past, and each other. It causes deep pain, cultural disintegration and sometimes death. As a Navajo

The Grand Carajas iron ore project replaces the rainforest.

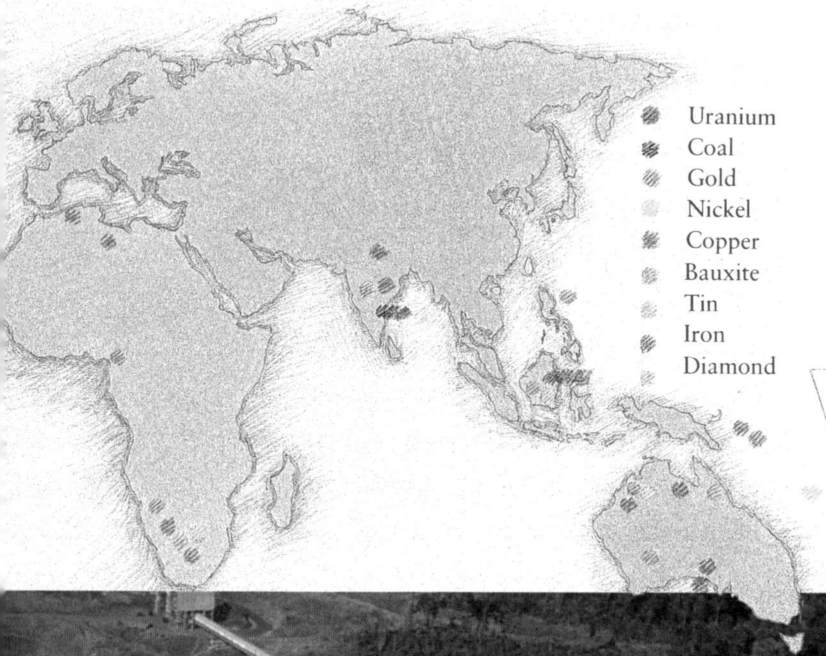

Uranium
Coal
Gold
Nickel
Copper
Bauxite
Tin
Iron
Diamond

The right to mine *Few
indigenous areas are free
from the threat of
mining. Nearly all states
protect their rights over
the subsoil, and in cases
of conflict will favour
mining. The map shows
major mining projects
on indigenous land.*

spokeswoman explained, *"When a person dies, we bury the body in the land and it turns into earth. So we can't leave our land; it would be like leaving our dead, our bodies. Because the earth is our mother. The liver of the earth is coal; the lung is uranium. Earthquakes and tornadoes are her breath. Now she's in pain. When the government takes her organs, she dies. The government only wants money. It doesn't think of her children: we people and the four-legged people who talk."*

Even more threatening can be the demands made on the land by the infrastructure and processing plants. Roads, railways, airstrips, power lines, and housing occupy greater areas of land than the mine itself. Huge energy demands, particularly for refining, often bring in new dam-building programmes, which displace more people. And while mining companies claim to rehabilitate mined-out sites, they often leave gaping holes, fail to neutralize toxic waste, and even where they plant grass or trees, these are usually inappropriate to the climate or the local communities.

Millions of indigenous people have lost their lands to mining in this century. Today hundreds of thousands are facing forced relocation. In the Black Mesa Mountains 20,000 Hopi and Navajo are being removed to make way for coal mining, and 10,000 more are threatened. The Greater Carajas projects in Brazil will affect 100,000 people, including 13,000 Indians. But resistance is growing, and indigenous people do not lack courage or resolve. *"What will the US goverment do to the Big Mountain people when it finally sinks in . . . that we will not move and that we will resist? Will members of our families be killed or sent to prison? . . . many of our people, many others, black, white and Indian will ask more questions. They will ask why didn't we hear about this issue?"* Navajo and Hopi statement

Spillover destruction *Up to 30 times as much land is taken up by infrastructure as by the mine itself (see diagram, above). Smelters for the Carajas iron ore project in eastern Amazonia will require an area of rainforest the size of Wisconsin. The project, financed by the World Bank, the European Community, and Japanese and German banks, will need 1.1 million tonnes of charcoal to fire the smelters and will run out of trees within 20 years. Hydroelectricity plants needed to power large mining projects often become part of even larger energy development programmes, which displace even more people.*

SACRED LAND, TWICE LOST?
Uranium in Western Australia

For many Aboriginal people of Western Australia, mining spells spiritual death. It removes them from the land entrusted to them in the Dreamtime (see pp. 70-1); it desecrates the sacred places that hold spiritual power; it denies them cultural integrity, and pollutes both land and people. *"When you take an Aboriginal man from his land, you take him from the spirit that is giving him life; that spirit cannot be regenerated in some other place. So you end up with shells of human beings, living in other peoples' countries."* Pat Dodson, Director of the Central Lands Council

Only 40 years ago, the 200 Martu people of Punmu and around the same number of Martu at Parngurr had little or no contact with white Australia. Ten years later the two communities were drawn out of the desert into Christian mission stations and the fringes of small mining towns. The elders saw their people becoming dependent on welfare, they watched the young losing their Manjiljarra language and turning to alcohol and petty crime.

In 1981, the elders decided to move the community back to their traditional lands. They are learning once again to live off the land, they have set up their own school, and are regaining their cultural identity. But they are threatened for a second time. In 1985 CRA Exploration, a subsidiary of Rio Tinto Zinc, discovered uranium near by. The company has taken out licences throughout the area and is poised for full-scale mining. If mining begins, it will not only endanger the ecosystem of the Rudall River but will pollute the water supply on which the communities depend for survival.

"These are our waterholes" *The drawing below depicts a waterhole and all the elements of Aboriginal life threatened by mining.* "We have a story for every waterhole. The younger generation want to know when we are dead and gone. We want to leave something behind for them. We have our own culture for the Martu. We are in the right place. We are not going to move out. We are going to settle down." *A member of the Punmu community*

BETTY WHYOULTER

GOLD DIGGERS
Mining on Yanomami land

Individual prospectors can be as damaging to indigenous peoples as multinational mining companies. In Brazil, it is the *garimpeiros*, small-scale gold miners, who are most active on Yanomami land. Since 1987 over 50,000 miners have poured in, clearing the forests, destroying the soil, diverting the rivers, and polluting them with mercury. Turning a blind eye to the enterprise are the armed forces, politicians, and businesspeople.

In December 1987 the Yanomami were on the point of securing legal recognition and protection for their lands. But their case clashed with the interests of the Calha Norte Plan, a national security project designed to establish a military presence along Brazil's northern border.

The armed forces installed military bases and landing strips along a 6600-km- (4000-mile-long) and 150-km- (100-mile-) wide area cutting across Yanomami land. However, the presence of the army has not discouraged the prospectors, who have built illegal runways. The *garimpeiros'* earnings, however, are linked to local businesses, including the local aircraft company, and 80 per cent of the gold now leaves the country illegally.

While the Yanomami were sole masters of their territory, frontier security was assured. Yet today, the region has become a "Wild West" of violence and lawlessness. The prospectors have killed Yanomami people, raped women, taken children, and stolen from their gardens. The game has fled from large parts of the forest, and the Yanomami are experiencing hunger. Most damaging of all are the imported diseases.

"I do not want gold prospectors here. I do not want my forest destroyed. I want to protect the Toucan, the river of my people. Your lands are already vast enough. Do not covet mine as well." Esmeraldo Tisibora-u-theri

Ruined lifestyle *This Yanomami drawing describes the delicate, efficient, and sustainable forest system that the gold prospectors are disrupting. The villages are linked by a network of paths, so that communities can meet and join together for food-gathering trips. After several years each community moves on, so that resources are not exhausted.*

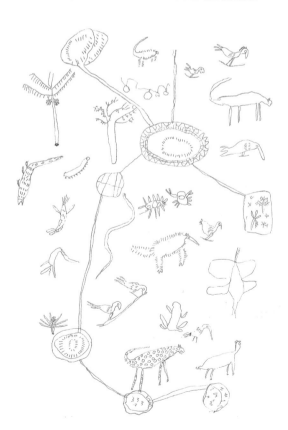

The mythical and historical heartland of Yanomami land lies in the Parima mountains, straddling the Brazil-Venezuela border.

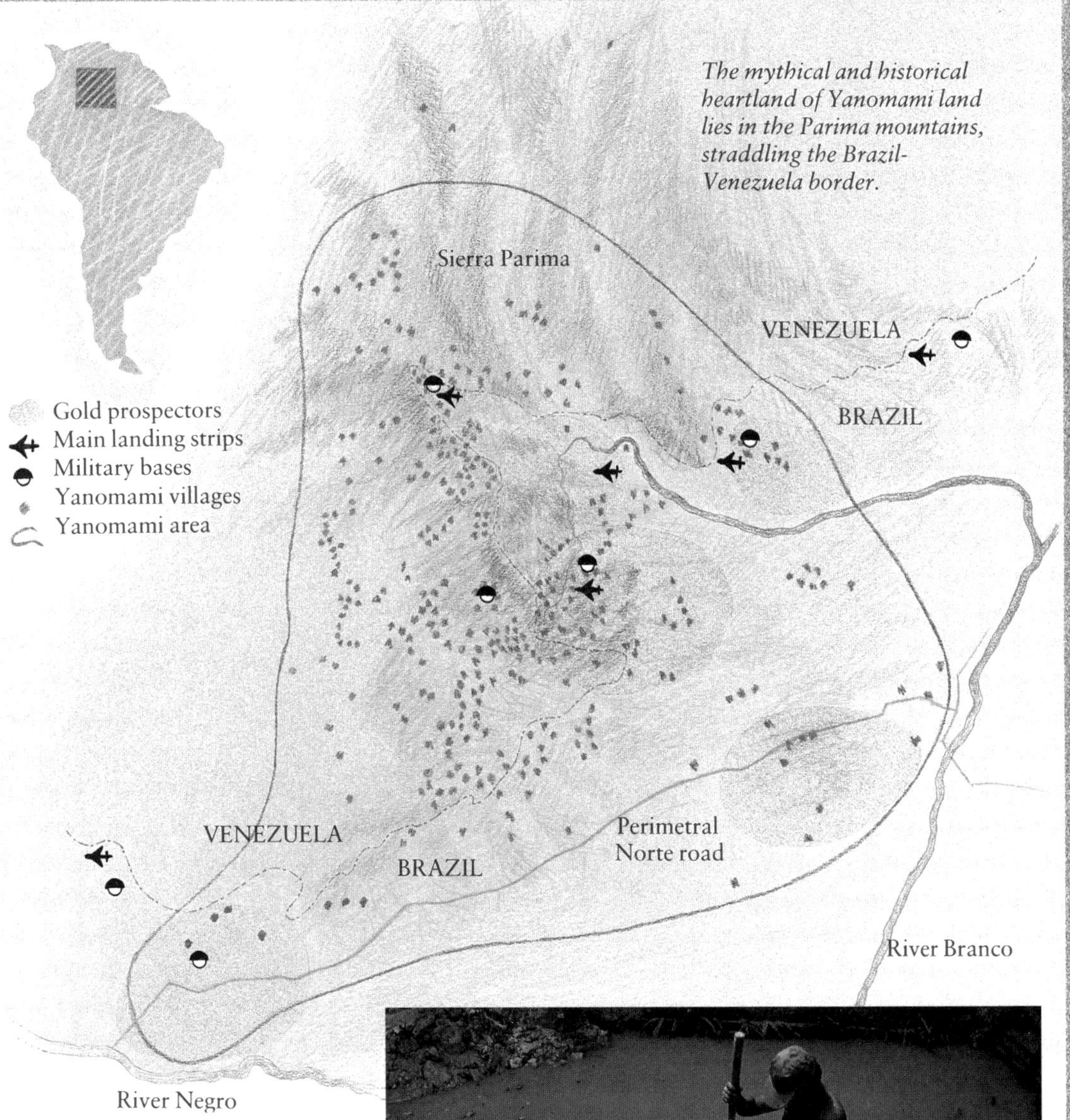

Sierra Parima

VENEZUELA

BRAZIL

Gold prospectors
Main landing strips
Military bases
Yanomami villages
Yanomami area

VENEZUELA

BRAZIL

Perimetral Norte road

River Branco

River Negro

Pits of pollution *New technology used in small-scale gold mining has increased disease and pollution. Hydraulic diggers sink pits to reach the water table and mines become muddy swamps where mosquitoes breed. Mercury sediments and human waste drain into local rivers, used by the Yanomami for fishing, bathing, and drinking.*

MILITARIZATION

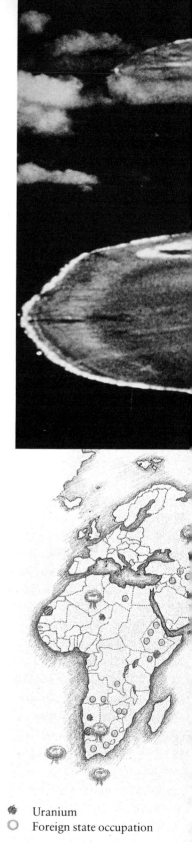

"The scientists, generals and leaders – recognized, paid, honored and treated as learned and knowledgeable men in this society, though obviously not necessarily wise men – are playing little boys' games with our lives and the lives of unborn generations of human, plant and animal life. These big boys are members of a special club based on power. They think in terms of moves and counter-moves, attack and retreat, winning and losing." Marie-Helen Laraque, Dene writer

Most of our contemporary conflicts directly affect indigenous peoples. The superpowers see their homelands as "empty territory" – testing grounds for nuclear and chemical weapons, bases for military installations, or a source of uranium, the raw material for nuclear weapons. Newly independent states wanting to establish their borders and develop their economies incorporate tribal territories as part of their nation-building efforts. Sometimes indigenous territories have been invaded and occupied for strategic and economic reasons. And when conflicts break out the superpowers are often involved.

    Since 1963, the US has exploded over 650 nuclear weapons in the Nevada Desert on western Shoshone territory. Early warning systems (DEWs), prime targets in case of war, are in place on Inuit lands in the Arctic. Cruise missiles are periodically test fired in Canada's Northwest Territories: they follow the Mackenzie River, the traditional hunting ground of

State or nation Of the 120 or more wars in the world today, 72% are conflicts between central state governments and a distinct nation of peoples living within its borders. The map shows military activity on indigenous land.

Bikini Island, Micronesia (top right), the target of over 20 nuclear explosions

    🌀 Uranium
    ○ Foreign state occupation

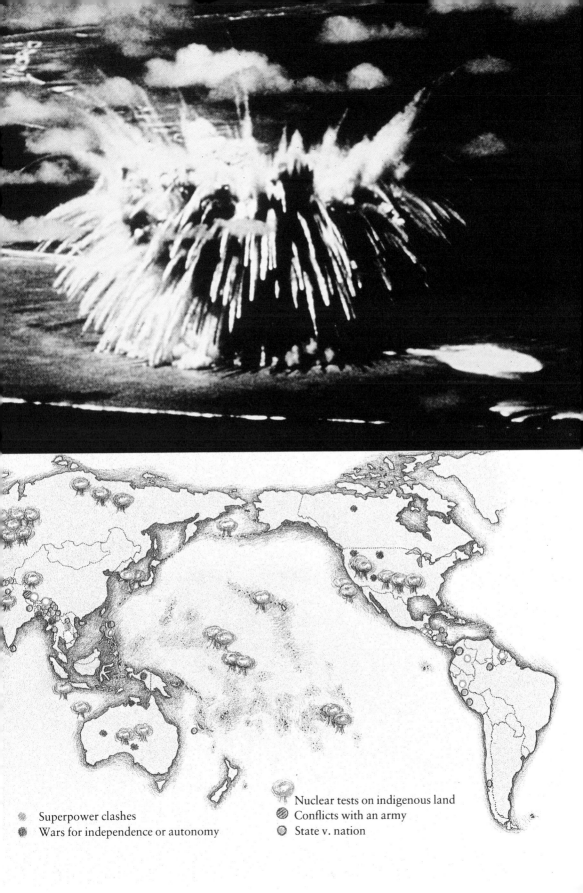

Superpower clashes
Wars for independence or autonomy

Nuclear tests on indigenous land
Conflicts with an army
State v. nation

the Cree and Dene, and finally drop into the Primrose Bombing Range in Saskatchewan, part of 1.2 million hectares of land belonging to the Cree in the 1940s, whose return they are still seeking.

The USSR has established military bases on indigenous land in eastern Siberia and the Soviet Far East. In China, the Uighur people claim that nuclear tests have caused premature deaths, deformed babies, and poisoned crops and pastures. Insufficient measures are taken to warn indigenous people of nuclear tests and protect them from the consequences.

The radiation released during nuclear testing damages the environment, contaminates the staple foods of indigenous people, and increases the risk of birth defects, miscarriages, sterility, cancer, and other diseases. After the atomic explosions on the Polynesian island of Bikini in the 1950s, 70 out of 1093 people died of cancer in three years.

Indigenous people are increasingly being drawn into violent local conflicts. The most prolonged and destructive of these have occurred following decolonization. Since World War II over 100 new states have emerged from the artificial national boundaries drawn by the retiring colonial powers, often with a dominant ethnic group becoming, in effect, the new colonial ruler (see pp. 86-7). In several countries – Myanmar (Burma), India, Bangladesh, Indonesia, Ethiopia, Sudan, Guatemala, and Nicaragua – indigenous people have taken up arms to defend themselves against government policies. In Myanmar (Burma) a 40-year-long war with the Karen, now united with other minority peoples, has claimed some 200,000 lives.

In some developing countries, indigenous peoples have tried to defend their lands against the threat of economic development or settlement. Violent confrontations took place, for example, in the Philippines when former President Marcos tried to build a series of dams in the Cordillera region in the 1970s. The armed forces committed numerous atrocities and indigenous people joined the New Peoples Army, the armed resistance movement.

HUMAN COST

Almost all nuclear tests have taken place on indigenous lands and waters.

Over 200,000 people died in Indonesia's invasion of East Timor.

The Karen of Myanmar (Burma) have been at war with the government since 1948.

Over 1 million people have been displaced because of violence in Guatemala.

Over 500,000 people have died in wars since 1945 in Indonesia, Ethiopia, India, and Pakistan.

There are well over 14 million international refugees, many of them displaced indigenous people.

Global military expenditure equals the total debt of the developing countries.

Over a million people have died in wars since 1945 in Bangladesh, Kampuchea, China, Vietnam, Korea, Nigeria, Iran, and Iraq.

The USA, Britain, and France have exploded over 215 nuclear bombs in the South Pacific.

China gives more military support to other nations than the USA or USSR.

IMPERIAL MATERIALISM
Chinese seizure of Tibet

Military annexation by a powerful neighbour can overturn the social and spiritual fabric as well as the economy of an indigenous population. Tibet, a Buddhist state with a central belief in nonviolence, is in the grip of a superpower: military occupation by the Chinese.

Since the Chinese Red Army invaded Tibet 40 years ago, it has destroyed land through mismanagement and dismantled what the Chinese considered to be feudal social relations, archaic economic practices, and an oppressive religion. They forced farmers to grow wheat instead of the better adapted hill barley. They collectivized herders and their animals. The result has been crop failures, overgrazing, and the first famine in the country's history. Up to 40 per cent of China's mineral wealth and most of its timber lies in Tibet. Billions of US dollars-worth of timber have been trucked to China.

The Chinese destroyed nearly all the 6000 monasteries and holy shrines and more than half the libraries. In 1959 10,000 Tibetans, including the Dalai Lama, Tibet's political and spiritual leader, fled to India. There are now well over 100,000 Tibetan refugees. Chinese immigration escalated in 1983, when the government offered Tibetan land to immigrants. The Tibetans who remain have been pushed up into the hills.

Tibet, bordering India, is a key part of China's defences, and China now keeps one-quarter of its nuclear force in the area. Chinese military presence has increased: today there is one soldier for every ten Tibetans.

Shifting borders *Little over half the original territory of Tibet is administered as the Tibetan Autonomous Region (TAR). The rest has been incorporated into four provinces of China. In Amdo, now part of Gansu, Sichuan, and Qinghai, there are 3.5 million Chinese to 700,000 Tibetans. In Lhasa, 75% of people are Chinese.*

①TAR
②Eastern Kham
③Amdo

1 million
▨ Chinese
▦ Tibetans
⌒ Old border

Crushing blow *Tibet's social, political and religious framework has been dismantled by the People's Republic of China since their invasion over 40 years ago, in 1950.*

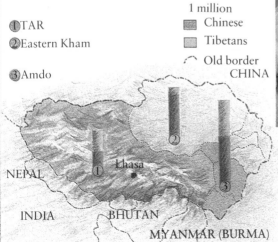

NEPAL   Lhasa   CHINA
INDIA   BHUTAN
MYANMAR (BURMA)

MILITARY PLAYGROUND
The Innu take on Nato

The territories of indigenous peoples are singled out for nuclear testing and training largely because of their relatively low population density. From atomic tests on Aboriginal land in Australia, to low-flying jets over the homes of the Innu in Labrador, Canada, military activity endangers the lives of indigenous peoples and those of the animals inhabiting the region.

Throughout 1988 and 1989 Innu people have been protesting against a NATO proposal to establish a $800 million "Tactical Fighter Weapons Training Centre" at Goose Bay. Innu land, known as Nitassinan, includes Goose Bay, and covers 100,000 sq km (40,000 sq miles) of Labrador and Quebec. The people have never agreed to Canadian sovereignty.

Until the 1950s, 10,000 Innu lived a nomadic, hunter-gatherer existence. The Americans built the air force base at Goose Bay in 1942, as a stopover point. But in 1980 European air forces started to practise low-level flying over Innu land. Jet bombers fly at 900km (550 miles) an hour, just 30m (100ft) above the ground. Flights have increased from 3000 sorties in 1984, to 7000 in 1988, and 40,000 are projected by 1992.

A further plan by NATO for six bombing ranges, will make hunting and fishing impossible in a large part of the Innu homeland. The Innu and their Inuit neighbours are caretakers of the George River caribou herd, the world's largest. Since the NATO flights began, the caribou population has declined dramatically. As Innu spokesperson, Daniel Ashini, sums up, *"We can't think of a worse desecration of our homeland than to have it used for war games".*

"The suddenness of the jet's arrival, and the deafening noise, take us by surprise and our hearts race and our bodies react in panic. The children cry out, our elders clutch their chests in fear. This is how the colonizers now attack our peaceful life in the interior." Innu spokesperson

Hunted by jets *The Innu herd of 600,000 caribou has approximately halved since the invasion by low-flying jets. The animals are thinner and less healthy, travelling 50 to 70km (30 to 40 miles) per day – about five times the original distance – before stopping to eat, to avoid the noise and pollution of the jets.*

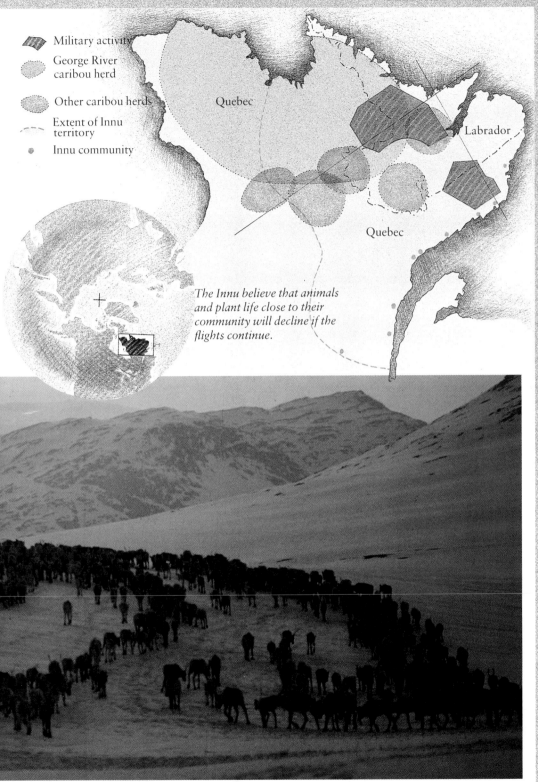

Military activity

George River
caribou herd

Other caribou herds

Extent of Innu
territory

Innu community

Quebec

Labrador

Quebec

*The Innu believe that animals
and plant life close to their
community will decline if the
flights continue.*

SITTING TARGETS FOR WORLD WAR
Militarization in the Pacific

The Pacific Ocean, separating the two superpowers, the USA and USSR, bristles with military bases and nuclear fleets. Since 1946 it has been the focus of nuclear tests and target practice and now the millions of islanders fear they may become targets for world war.

The political boundaries of the Pacific islands create a patchwork of ownership. But resistance to militarization and political subjugation is growing: a number of Pacific peoples have won or are seeking independence.

Many of the Pacific islands are governed by other powers: USA, France, Britain, and New Zealand. Others are independent; some of these have entered agreements with the great powers to host defence activities. The USA has 167 military installations and bases in the Pacific; France has 15 and the presence of both is increasing.

The effect on the islands is colossal, particularly from French and US activities. The French have detonated 100 nuclear devices above and, since 1975, below ground. Missiles are launched from the USA into the Marshall Islands; a US Star Wars development is now underway on the island of Kwajalein; one third of Guam is occupied with US installations. Most of the 100,000 Chamorro Islanders on Guam depend on state welfare after losing their prime agricultural land.

Radioactive fall-out after US tests on Rongelap Atoll meant that the islands had to be abandoned. And, despite official reassurances, radioactive iodine has been found at Moruroa Lagoon following French experiments. Leukaemia, thyroid cancer, stillbirths, and foetal malformations have increased among people living in the vicinity of the test areas.

Inherited suffering *The devastation from the testing, sickness, the seizure of lands, the build-up of military installations: these were the immediate repercussions of the nuclear experiments. Later came the disabling genetic tragedies such as this child with malformed limbs (below). Stillbirths and malformations, leukaemia, tumours, and a host of minor complications have beset the islanders.*

The islanders *The Pacific, covering almost one-third of the globe, is home to six million indigenous people. They are traditionally grouped into Melanesians, who constitute 80 per cent of the population, Micronesians, and Polynesians. Few, if any, remain unaffected by military activity.*

"They say the US military will defend Belau . . . I don't believe the US military's interest in Belau is for the defence of the Belauans. I believe it's for the defence of the United States . . I don't believe we make peace by fighting war . . ." Lorenza Pedro, a Belauan woman, speaking in London in 1986

The damage so far *The USA, Britain, and France have exploded more than 200 nuclear bombs in the South Pacific. In the Marshall Islands, 66 bombs were detonated between 1946 and 1962. Fourteen islands were left uninhabitable and six islands completely destroyed.*

French testing *France has used Moruroa Atoll, southeast of Tahiti in French Polynesia, for tests since 1966. From 1966 to 1975, 41 atmospheric tests were conducted there and at Fangataufa Atoll. When France started testing on Moruroa it stopped releasing statistics on mortality and causes of death in French Polynesia.*

Dumping waste *Nuclear and chemical waste has been dumped in the seas by Britain, USA, and Japan without acceptable guarantees for its safety. Britain, USA, France, Switzerland, and South Africa voted against a ban on nuclear dumping at sea. Japan abstained. Sub-seabed emplacement is currently being researched, but the dangers of an unstable ocean floor and fluctuating temperatures make this a highly dangerous option.*

CLASH OF CULTURES
Refugees from Bangladesh

Genocide is an act designed to bring about the deliberate destruction, in whole or in part, of an ethnic, racial, or religious group. The tribal people of the Chittagong Hill Tracts in Bangladesh, witnessing whole communities killed, see themselves as victims of an undeclared war, some even call it genocide.

In 1963 pressure was placed on the Chittagong Hill Tracts when 100,000 hill people were forced further into the hills because their land was flooded by a large reservoir, which drowned 40 per cent of the area's arable soil. One year later the government of Bangladesh allowed Bengali peasants into the area, enticed by offers of free land. Their harvests failed after tools and seed supplies promised by the government did not materialize. The settlers resorted to stealing from their tribal neighbours. At the same time, self-government was taken away from the tribal people. The interests of the hill tribes and the peasants were then at odds.

The Muslim newcomers considered the Buddhist and animist indigenous inhabitants backward and primitive. They mocked the tribal women. Fights broke out and killings began. The Bangladesh army moved in to protect the government-sponsored settlers and the tribespeople were massacred.

In the mid-1970s, after repeated appeals to the government had been ignored, the hill people began an armed resistance. The government sent in more troops and strengthened the police force. Violence in the forms of torture, rape, the burning of villages, and pillage persists against the hill tribes, and about 50,000 refugees have fled into neighbouring India.

The Chittagong Hill Tracts cover an area of 1.6 million hectares. Over half the land is forested and only 20% is suitable for cultivation. Occupying the southeastern corner of Bangladesh, many of the hill tribespeople live in valleys, the rest occupy forested hill ridges.

Escape route *An elderly hill tribeswoman is carried to a forest hide-out to escape attack from Bengali peasants. Already over 50,000 people from the hill tracts – nearly 10% of the tribal population – have fled to refugee camps in India.*

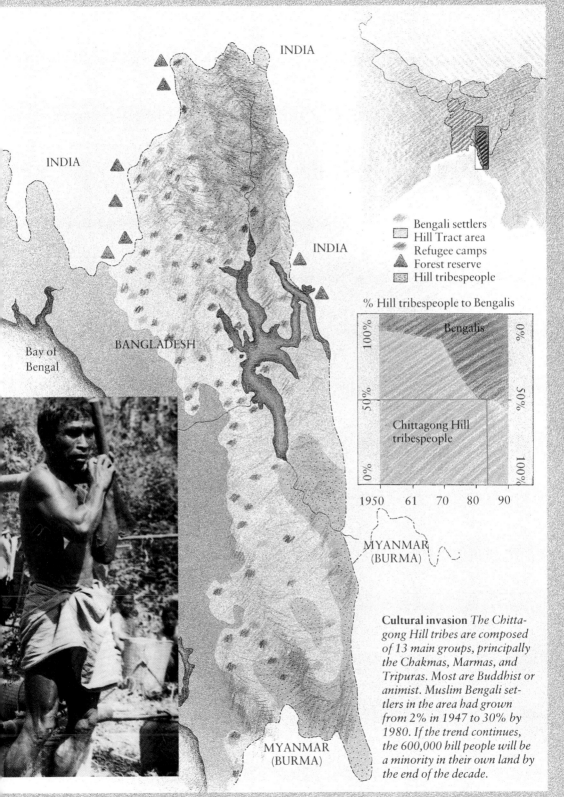

INDIA

INDIA

INDIA

INDIA

BANGLADESH

Bay of
Bengal

MYANMAR
(BURMA)

MYANMAR
(BURMA)

Bengali settlers
Hill Tract area
Refugee camps
Forest reserve
Hill tribespeople

% Hill tribespeople to Bengalis

Bengalis

Chittagong Hill
tribespeople

100% 50% 0%

0% 50% 100%

0% 50% 100%

1950   61   70   80   90

Cultural invasion *The Chitta-gong Hill tribes are composed of 13 main groups, principally the Chakmas, Marmas, and Tripuras. Most are Buddhist or animist. Muslim Bengali settlers in the area had grown from 2% in 1947 to 30% by 1980. If the trend continues, the 600,000 hill people will be a minority in their own land by the end of the decade.*

OVERLAPPING BOUNDARIES
Strife in Ethiopia

Almost all African states are multi-national and, while a single group often holds power, in most countries it is not the majority population. National frontiers laid down by European colonizers largely ignored the boundaries of indigenous peoples. Consequently, many groups straddle frontiers, and are administered by more than one government.

Ethiopia, beset by drought and famine, is torn by wars of national liberation. The orthodox Christian Amharic people dominate political life but constitute only 15 per cent of the population.

The Oromo make up half of Ethiopia's population, but have virtually no say in national affairs. They lost their best lands to the ruling powers in the last century; their religion was outlawed, and they lost the right to be taught their own language at school. Many are recruited into the army against their will. In the mid-1970s the Oromo Liberation Front was launched. Since then the government has moved more than 6 million Oromo into army-controlled villages.

In the 1960s, Eritrea was given autonomy within a federated Ethiopia. Soon after, this was subverted. Protest led to armed resistance.

The boundaries of the Somali people stretch into Kenya and Ethiopia, but the Ethiopian war in 1977 precluded contact with those pastoralist Somali still within the Ethiopian boundaries.

The tragic effects of these wars in Ethiopa include 3 to 4 million men at arms, 1 million internal refugees, and an impoverished state on the edge of starvation.

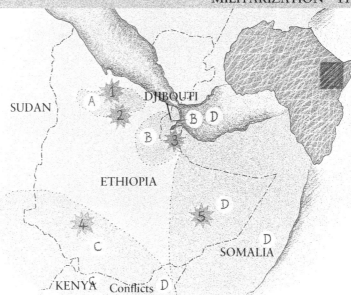

In sub-Saharan Africa, more than 450 million people live in fewer than 50 states. 1800 languages with 2500 dialects are represented. State boundaries do not reflect the natural boundaries of the indigenous groups. Liberation movements represent the struggle to reinstate the original frontiers.

Guerrilla celebrations
Soldiers from the Eritrean People's Liberation Front celebrate the retaking of towns from government forces (left).

Sedentarization Africa's most threatened peoples are those living in remote areas, where the land is unsuitable for settled agriculture (below). African governments have tried to sedentarize the nomadic pastoralists, and hunters and gatherers, thus creating an uncertain future for them. The use of the plough on marginal agricultural land can destroy the top soil and render the soil useless for cultivation, turning previously productive areas into desert.

Conflicts
1   Eritrean Liberation Front
    Eritrean People's Liberation Front
2   Tigray People's Liberation Front
3   Afar People
4   Western Somali Liberation Front
5   Oromo Liberation Front
Peoples
A   Tigray
B   Afar
C   Oromo
D   Somali

THE ENVIRONMENTAL THREAT

*"Let me ask you this – why are there
only 8 inches of top-soil left in
America, when there once were some
18 inches at the time of the
Declaration of Independence in
1776? Where goes our sacred earth?"*
Hobart Keith, Oglala Sioux

The cumulative effect of forest loss, mining, dams,
military activity, and industrialization is driving the
planet to the limit.

We are losing around 30 hectares of tropical
forest every minute. Over 15 million hectares – an
area nearly four times the size of Switzerland –
disappears every year. Sometimes more. In 1988, an
area of Amazonia equivalent to Belgium went up in
smoke within months. These forest fires release
carbon dioxide into the atmosphere. Emissions of
chlorofluorocarbons (CFCs) and fossil fuels are
adding to the greenhouse effect and eating away the
protective ozone layer. One-third of the world's
arable land is disintegrating into desert. In the
tropics the major wetland ecosystems look set to
disappear in less than a decade. Droughts, floods,
and climate shifts are already symptoms of more
serious, permanent climate changes to come. And
scientists calculate that at the current rate of
deforestation 50 to 100 species could be lost every
day.

Indigenous people live in these fragile
environments and are the first to suffer the effects of
this war on the ecosystem. Their close relationship
with the natural world leaves them particularly
vulnerable. Large-scale logging leaves them no
forest and thin soils which are soon leached by the
tropical rains. Mercury used by gold prospectors in
Amazonia has poisoned as much as 1500km (930
miles) of their river system, killing fish and causing
illness among thousands of Indians. About 5 million
tonnes of toxic waste, including fluoride emissions
from aluminium smelting are dumped daily into the
St Lawrence river, Cañada, causing miscarriages,
birth defects, and cancer among Mohawk Indians.
Indigenous people of the Pacific (and Arctic) have

Forest fires *Even if forest fires,
as those in Brazil (right), and
the use of fossil fuels stopped
tomorrow, the warming effect
of past CO_2 emissions and
other greenhouse gases, such as
methane, would be felt for
decades.*

Drought *Global warming is
already bringing a more unstable climate, and more
droughts, such as the 1988
parching of the US corn belt,
and the Sahel (right), as well as
more floods, freezing, and hur-
ricanes, are predicted.*

Floods *As global warming causes sea levels to rise, flooding, as in the Sudan (centre left), will increase existing pressure on the land.*

borne the brunt of the dumping of radioactive waste (as well as nuclear testing). Johnson Island, home to 90,000 Pacific islanders, is the site of a US toxic waste incinerator. Toxic emissions leak into the sea, polluting the entire food chain.

When indigenous people protest against environmental destruction, they are protecting not just themselves, but all humanity and the 10 to 30 million other species. For increasing changes to the climate, air, soil, and water – the basic ingredients of life – threaten the existence of all inhabitants of this planet.

CULTURAL COLLAPSE

"Next to shooting indigenous peoples, the surest way to kill us is to separate us from our part of the Earth. Once separated, we will either perish in body or our minds and spirits will be altered so that we end up mimicking foreign ways, adopt foreign languages, accept foreign thoughts . . . Over time, we lose our identity and . . . eventually die or are crippled as we are stuffed under the name of 'assimilation' into another society."
Hayden Burgess, World Council of Indigenous Peoples

The land is the physical and spiritual core that binds communities together. When indigenous peoples lose their land, they lose their language, their complex social and political systems, and their knowledge. At a deeper level traditions are eroded with their sacred beliefs. Although some may integrate and recover meaning to their lives, the removal of first peoples from their land can be likened to genocide in slow motion.

The young are drawn to the Western way of life, but sometimes internalize hostile attitudes. They grow ashamed of their indigenous status and reject the values of their elders. Caught between two cultures, they seek escape from their loss of native identity through crime, alcohol, drugs, sometimes suicide; in Canada, the suicide rate of young Indians is seven times the national average. To survive at all they must adopt Western values.

Such loss of identity is accelerated by loss of language. Indigenous languages are rarely, if ever, given legal recognition and in many cases are banned in schools. Less than five per cent of Maori school children now speak their own language. In Canada, Cree children in the past forbidden to

"As we approach the 21st century (as the White man reckons time), we Indians are desperately seeking ways to maintain our tribal identities and ways to survive as distinct cultural entities." Reuben Snake, Winnebago Indian

"An Indian without land is a dead Indian and an ethnic community without a language is a dying community." Rodolfo Stavenhagen

"The Indians used to laugh much more! Now they're depressed. The only time they seem to laugh is when they drink." Peter Matthiessen, Indian Country

"We do not wish to destroy your religion, or take it from you. We only want to enjoy our own." Red Jacket, Iroquois

"How can you respect yourself if you don't know who you are? I have taught my children the only way I know which was the way my mother taught me and I have lived it to the best of my ability. The quality of future life depends on how we demonstrate our beliefs to our children."
Marie Wilson, elder of the Gitksan Nation

■

"Without my language I couldn't possibly understand my culture and its values. I was denied what is essentially a basic human right – access to myself. Now we've got to change that." Cathy Dewes, Maori teacher

■

"When an Aboriginal man or woman cannot walk into a hotel or a shop or anywhere without getting stared at, without getting called, 'black bastards, coons, heathens, savages, lazy, shiftless, stupid, dirty, filthy niggers' – this is violence."
Gwalwa Daraniki Association

"I remember my mother very well. She used to sit there smoking a pipe, sewing and chatting to us about a variety of things in our own language. My father would wake me early in the morning and we would go fishing. I used to wade into the water up to my waist to scoop up the salmon he would catch. Then we would go home and teach the younger ones how to clean the fish. Then my father would sing and dance." Susie Bear, 1988

■

"only the white . . . think that their race has the key to cultural development, or that we, only by intermarrying with them, can improve our quality as human beings. This way of thinking is a totally outrageous offence to the dignity of our people."
Council of Amant'as, Bolivia

WHILE THEY WERE SO BUSY MOLDING ME, THEY FORGOT ONE THING...

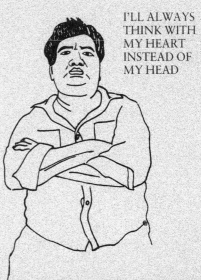

I'LL ALWAYS THINK WITH MY HEART INSTEAD OF MY HEAD

speak their own language at school developed psychological and learning problems. Language is a means of transmitting oral knowledge of myths, history, cultural tradition, and the natural world. By separating young children from their parents the destructive process of assimilation has been accelerated. In Indonesia the government has declared it will remove tribal children from their homes "to keep them from settling into their parents' lifestyle".

Missionary childhood

"The other children were taken into the residential school at 5 and 6 years. I was lucky, I went at 9. And my grandmother raised me in the traditional way, so I had a strong sense of identity. I only spoke Cree, not a word of English.

In the school we were not allowed to speak our own language or practise our religion. Nor were we allowed to talk to our own relatives, especially the boys. The ceremonies we have at the age of puberty which celebrate the change from childhood to adulthood were denied us. It was as if we were not human beings. We are a very affectionate people; we walk arm in arm and so on. These gestures were completely forbidden. They did their best to make you lose your self-esteem, your sense of being Indian.

When we did not obey the rules we were hit and pushed and shouted at. This was a shock because in our community we do not raise our voice at children or hit them. And to punish us they would cut our hair because they know it would bring shame for a long time. So we were afraid even to speak our language.

Under the treaties, schools had been set up on reserves, but the missionaries complained that we kept up our old ways, spoke our own language, practised our religion. So in 1886 the government established residential schools a long way from the reserves to make sure we were assimilated. For the next 80 years all Indian children from the age of 6 to 16 were taken from their families and brought up in these institutions run by the Churches. In 1969 the system was ended but the nightmare goes on. Even today, when I see a nun I freeze inside. The legacy is with us still. We are dealing with the problems today; people who have lost direction, had their culture denigrated. Of the group of girls in my grade at the residential school, only I am still alive. I am 38 years old."

Sharon Venne, Cree, 1988

SCAPEGOATS OF THE DRUG TRADE
Opium and the Hmong of Thailand

Since drugs have become big business, indigenous people have been drawn into producing increasing amounts of the raw materials. The Hmong of Thailand and the Amazonian Indians of Colombia have become scapegoats, blamed for heroin and cocaine addiction problems which exist in richer countries.

- Towns
- Hmong villages
- Mountains

The highly distinctive Hmong are accomplished musicians and story-tellers and wear elaborately embroidered costumes. Opium poppies cultivated by the Hmong were traditionally grown for home consumption, smoked socially, and used to relieve pain, treat dysentery, and contain tuberculosis. As a cash crop, opium paid for silver, the traditional marriage offering to a bride's family.

British and French colonial powers began the large-scale exportation of opium as early as the 18th century. Today the USA provides the largest market, but the importation of opium and its derivative, heroin, is now illegal. Yet drug barons and corrupt police officials encourage opium cultivation and offer protection from Thai and US government attempts to stem the flow.

Alternative cash crops are susceptible to bad weather and fluctuating market prices. Profits rarely cover the cost of transportation to market.

The Hmong are blamed by the government for the rise in heroin addiction, yet for each dollar they receive 3000 are paid on the streets of New York. The trade persists mainly because of the lack of political will to deal with the profits made by dealers, who still find channels open for its supply.

Of 6 million Hmong, 58,000 live in northern Thailand in part of the world's prime opium area, the "Golden Triangle". The rest inhabit the highlands of southwestern China, Laos, and Vietnam.

Harvesting opium *Each ripe poppy head must be incised, the sap later scraped and gathered. Destroying the poppy fields alone cannot prevent the cultivation of the crop: as little as 50 sq km (20 sq miles) could supply the entire US heroin market.*

DEATHS IN CUSTODY
Racism and Australian Aborigines

We are not all equal in the eyes of the law, and it is indigenous people who suffer most. The rate of imprisonment for Canadian Indians is three times that for whites. In parts of New Zealand, Maoris make up 50 per cent of prisoners, even though they are only 9 per cent of the population. Australian jails have an Aboriginal intake 14 times the national average. And a disturbing number of Aborigines die in custody.

Aborigines suffered from European settlement: tens of thousands were shot, tortured, and poisoned as they resisted invasion. The violence continues as protective legislation for Aborigines has been ignored and as the police deal with the victims of acculturation.

Between 1980 and 1988, 103 Aborigines died in custody, according to a Royal Commission. Some died from natural causes, but nearly two-thirds of those under 30 who died were found hanged. Two or more Aborigines are now dying in custody every month. Aborigines allege that police or prison officers have been negligent or, in some cases, directly caused a death. The beating and subsequent death of 16-year-old John Pat at the hands of the police was witnessed in 1983. During the inquest, one detective admitted that police had falsified records. Five policemen charged with manslaughter were acquitted by an all-white jury.

Whether suicides or victims of violence, the root cause lies in the loss of Aboriginal land, citizenship, culture, and dignity.

The shadow of celebration *At the same time that white Australia celebrated 200 years of settlement Aboriginal deaths in custody became the country's biggest human rights issue. Most are found hanged. Since the invasion by Europeans, Aboriginal families have been forced from their lands, their rights and laws disregarded.*

Unwilling victims *Police arrest 1 million Aborigines each year – an average of four times a year for every Aboriginal man, woman, and child. Young men are often imprisoned for minor offences such as drunkenness or non-payment of fines – crimes often ignored when committed by non-Aborigines.*

"My race is psychologically scarred, and such condition is a direct result of the dispossession of our traditional lands, the destruction of our culture and the erosion of our customs. This has sapped our dignity and self-respect, and until such time as justice has been achieved in this area we will continue to crowd Australian prisons." Senator Neville Bonner, 1982

FORCED CONFORMITY
Post-Revolution USSR

The Russian Revolution of 1917 attempted to cast off the shackles of the oppressive regime of the Czars. But for more than one million indigenous peoples in the north and Siberia, this was only the first stage in the destruction of their ways of life. To what extent can the recent moves toward self-management and decentralization of power revive the independent development of the indigenous population?

Timber and mineral deposits in relatively isolated regions of the USSR were enormously attractive to the new Bolshevik government. The land was rapidly colonized. Forests were destroyed, rivers polluted, and pasturelands became flooded.
   In the 1930s, Stalin's government introduced collectivization programmes in agriculture. The reindeer herders of the north, such as the Chukchi, slaughtered their animals rather than allow them to join state farms. The number of domesticated reindeer fell by nearly one-third between 1929 and 1933. Children were sent to boarding schools to learn the Russian language, not their mother tongue. As a result, strong family and kin relations have been broken. Only a notional protection for indigenous groups, or "small peoples", has been allowed. Like many assimilated peoples, their health record is poor and unemployment is high. Domestic crime, drunkenness, and suicide are three to four times the national average.

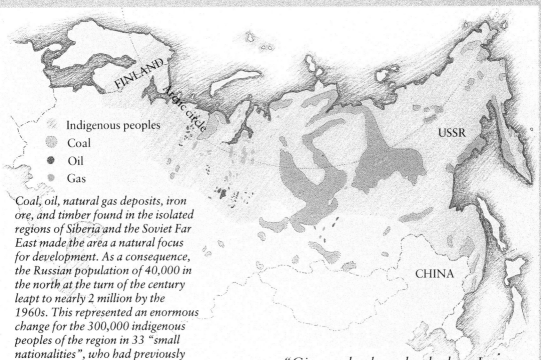

Indigenous peoples
Coal
Oil
Gas

FINLAND
Arctic circle
USSR
CHINA

Coal, oil, natural gas deposits, iron ore, and timber found in the isolated regions of Siberia and the Soviet Far East made the area a natural focus for development. As a consequence, the Russian population of 40,000 in the north at the turn of the century leapt to nearly 2 million by the 1960s. This represented an enormous change for the 300,000 indigenous peoples of the region in 33 "small nationalities", who had previously been the majority in the area.

"Give me back my land where I can graze my reindeers, hunt game and catch fish. Give me my land where my deers are not attacked by stray dogs, where my hunting trails are not trampled down by poachers or fouled by vehicles, where the rivers and lakes have no oil slicks. I want land where my home, my sanctuary and graveyard can remain inviolable. I want land where I cannot be robbed of my clothes or boots in broad daylight. Give me my own land, not someone else's. Just a tiny patch of my own land." Khanty reindeer herder, in Moscow News Weekly No.2 1989

Reversing the programme *A reform process, known as "perestroika", has recently begun, which aims to restructure the economy, largely through decentralization and de-collectivization. Boarding schools established under Stalin's rule may now be closed.*

DEAD-END JOBS
Tourism in Hawaii

Intensive tourism in Hawaii over several decades has forced local inhabitants to give up their lands and traditional way of life. In the words of a protester, *"Tourism is the lowest paying and largest dead-end-jobs industry in the state . . . it's time to fight back!"*

Since World War II tourism has transformed Hawaii. By 1988 6.5 million people were flooding into the resorts, bringing $9.2 million per year. More jobs and a better standard of living were promised, but the unemployment rate quadrupled between 1940 and 1980. Native Hawaiians found few openings except in low-paid jobs with few prospects in hotels and laundries. Land speculation and a housing shortage meant that for most Hawaiians a family home was completely out of the question.

   Tourism has also ruined the environment and made the traditional way of life impossible. It has brought highways, cars, and airports. Luxury liners empty raw sewage and oil into the Pacific Ocean. Mud run-off from land developments and white silt from dredged coral reefs cover the sea floor, killing the food supply for marine animals, poisoning fish, and destroying the livelihoods of native fishing families. "Venetian gondolas" now float on mullet ponds that once fed people. If native Hawaiians practise their traditional fishing and gathering lifestyle they are prosecuted. Many sacred native burial areas and archeological sites are now parks and restaurants. Local people are stared at from tour buses as though they are zoo animals.

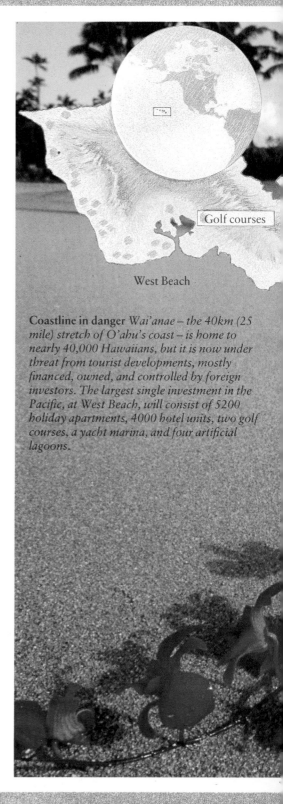

West Beach

Golf courses

Coastline in danger *Wai'anae – the 40km (25 mile) stretch of O'ahu's coast – is home to nearly 40,000 Hawaiians, but it is now under threat from tourist developments, mostly financed, owned, and controlled by foreign investors. The largest single investment in the Pacific, at West Beach, will consist of 5200 holiday apartments, 4000 hotel units, two golf courses, a yacht marina, and four artificial lagoons.*

Homes for golf courses *Local residents demonstrate to save their homes — due to be razed to make way for new tourist developments.*

MISSIONARY ZEAL
Evangelists in Paraguay

Fundamentalist Protestant missions such as the Summer Institute of Linguistics and the New Tribes Mission (NTM) believe that indigenous people are merely heathens awaiting conversion to the missionaries' god. Governments, notably in Latin America and Asia, have given their blessing to the missionary presence, thereby often destroying indigenous ways of life and opening the territory to oil men, loggers, and cattle ranchers.

The Florida-based New Tribes Mission works with five tribes in Paraguay, attacking their villages and removing them to mission bases. Those who survive the change in diet, contact with previously unknown diseases, inadequate medical attention, and the trauma of contact, are rapidly introduced to a new language, a new religion, and cash payments for work.

The New Tribes Mission uses "tame" Indians to bring in forest groups. Ahinacay, a Totobiegosode Indian, was one of nine used to approach an uncontacted community of related Totobiegosode. Fearing an attack, the forest people prepared an ambush and attacked the mission Indians, killing five of them, including Ahinacay, whose shorn hair and Western clothing identified him as an "enemy". The NTM proclaimed him a "martyr for Christ", but Ahinacay had joined the mission party not out of a wish to convert, but only to renew contact with his family.

Following the clash, the forest people were taken to the NTM base at Campo Loro. Several have died there since. Survivors work for white settlers, who have taken over the Indians' forest lands.

Ethnocide is the systematic and deliberate destruction of a culture. Once demoralized by their dependence on the missionaries, tribal people assume alien notions of duty, family, good, and evil, which split apart a society that has developed a complex and self-sufficient way of life.

Four steps to ethnocide

○ **Contact** Missionaries leave gifts for indigenous peoples or use "tame" Indians to make initial contact.

○ **Dependency** Missionaries treat indigenous peoples as children. Dependency increases as the missionaries often provide some real improvements in health care and nutrition.

○ **Breakdown** Persuasion, bribery, and force are used to denigrate indigenous customs. Customary behaviour is outlawed and children are separated from their parents so that they learn to be "civilized".

○ **Indoctrination** The narrow norms of the missionaries are foisted on the demoralized Indians. They are taught to respect the Church, work for money, obey the boss, live in small family units, and wear Western clothes.

Worldwide network *The New Tribes Mission has over 2500 missionaries and a budget of $20 million for "tribal evangelism and indigenous church planting". It has been expelled from some Latin American countries, but still operates in 24 others worldwide, undermining the belief systems of indigenous peoples.*

Prostitution *Ayoreo Indian women, sometimes from the mission bases, find work with the newcomers who migrate into the land opened up by missionaries.*

PART THREE

ALIANÇA DOS POVOS DA FLORESTA

As populações tradicionais que hoje marcam no céu da Amazônia a área da Aliança dos Povos da Floresta proclamam seu vínculo de permanecer com suas regiões preservadas. Entendem que o desenvolvimento das potencialidades destas populações e das regiões em que habitam se constitui na economia futura de suas comunidades, e deve ser assegurado por toda nação brasileira como parte de sua afirmação e orgulho. Esta Aliança dos Povos da Floresta resolveu todos, seringueiros e ribeirinhos iniciada no Acre estende os braços para acolher todo esforço de proteção e preservação deste imenso povoamento sistema de vida que somos imensa florestas, lagos, rios e amazônias, tanta de nossas riquezas a base de nossas culturas e tradições.

CONSELHO NACIONAL DOS SERINGUEIROS
UNIÃO DAS NAÇÕES INDÍGENAS - UNI

ALTERNATIVE VISIONS

Indigenous peoples are increasingly active on the world
stage – fighting for self-determination, legal rights to land,
and the preservation of the environment, with strength,
imagination, and success. And they are now part of a larger
alliance concerned about the future. Human rights and
development organizations, environmentalists, scientists,
political parties and individuals see the important role
indigenous peoples are playing in the current ecological
crisis. Together they are challenging destructive models
of development. Damaging projects have not ceased, but
international banks, corporations, and governments are
now more ready to listen to indigenous peoples. The way
forward is not easy. Many indigenous peoples remain
unaware of the forces that threaten them, and there are
inevitable conflicts among those who have organized
successfully. Some peoples give priority to the education
of their young, others to sustainable development projects,
others to political lobbying. But a powerful process is in
motion. Growing numbers are dealing creatively with
external interests impinging on their world – winning back
their lands, running their own affairs, developing strategies
to sustain the rain forests, conserve the Arctic, create a
nuclear-free Pacific, and to come together peacefully to
ensure a future for all our children.

RESISTANCE

"Now we shall not rest until we have regained our rightful place. We shall tell our young people what we know. We shall send them to the corners of the earth to learn more. They shall lead us." Declaration of the Five County Cherokees

Indigenous peoples are not passive victims. Nor have they ever been. In the past they resisted colonialism through negotiation, political protest, civil disobedience, or force of arms. Sometimes they succeeded, sometimes they won partial guarantees of their territory, and sometimes they were overwhelmed by numbers and superior military technology. But the resistance has not stopped. Today's movement is part of this continuing process, and the struggle to survive as a people is as urgent as ever.

In the early days of European settlement in North America, the indigenous inhabitants could have defeated the vulnerable colony, but instead offered support with food and supplies. In Central America, Cortés too found allies, but in this case among those oppressed by the Aztecs. In Australia, the invaders were simply ignored by the Aborigines. But when the invading powers began to seize indigenous lands, and dismantle political and legal systems, they met with fierce resistance. In North America, the Indian nations held back colonialism for three centuries. In Australia, the Aborigines waged a long, guerrilla war against supply lines and property. In Latin America, Quechua-speaking peoples rose up against the Spanish invaders in the 1770s and 1780s. In India, the British Raj faced several rebellions by Santals, Mundas, and others.

Today's indigenous peoples are adopting modern and creative political techniques – using the media, joining forces, and gaining support from the wider community. Recently, indigenous peoples have scored some important victories. They have stopped harmful development projects, established their own political and welfare organizations, and regained rights usurped over the decades.

The Sioux story The Sioux War is one of the best-known acts of defence by indigenous peoples. In the 1860s the Sioux and their allies defeated government forces in the Powder River War and gained a large independent territory, guaranteed by the Treaty of Laramie. Four years later the government asked to build a railway track across the land. Chiefs Sitting Bull (right) and Crazy Horse rejected the request. But in 1874 the army was back. Meanwhile, illegal

The Mapuche fight back The Mapuche of Chile have a long history of resistance. They held off the southward expansion of the Inca empire, and defended their land from the Spanish. In a rare treaty, they secured 10 million hectares of their homeland, and kept settlers out for two centuries until the independent Chilean state crushed them in the 1880s. In the 1960s the Mapuche were back. They were promised extensive land, but received only 1500 hectares. Then under Allende's brief government in the early 1970s, they were at the forefront of a campaign for radical agrarian reform. 70,000 hectares of land were returned. But under the Pinochet dictatorship leaders were imprisoned and killed, and lands reduced to a fraction – legislation turned collectively owned indigenous lands into individual properties. Today, Mapuche organizations are an integral part of the alliance working for a new democracy. In 1989 they formed their own party.

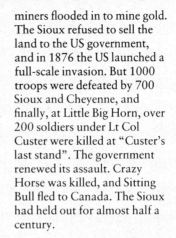

miners flooded in to mine gold. The Sioux refused to sell the land to the US government, and in 1876 the US launched a full-scale invasion. But 1000 troops were defeated by 700 Sioux and Cheyenne, and finally, at Little Big Horn, over 200 soldiers under Lt Col Custer were killed at "Custer's last stand". The government renewed its assault. Crazy Horse was killed, and Sitting Bull fled to Canada. The Sioux had held out for almost half a century.

The Chipko movement In 1972 Indian tribal women began the tree-hugging (Chipko) movement – a revival of an ancient non-violent protest to protect trees from the axe (right). It has now spread throughout the Himalayas, into other parts of India and beyond – as far as Scandinavia. The movement was inspired by the action of women in 1730, when over 300 followers of a Hindu sect who had pledged to cut no green trees nor kill any wild animals, were cut down as they hugged their trees. The current movement has won a moratorium on felling trees above 1000m and on 30° slopes for commercial purposes in Uttar Pradesh. Villagers who depend on the forest are aware of the importance of trees for maintaining water tables and river courses, and preventing soil erosion. *"Chipko is a revolt against the existing values which regard Nature as a commodity."*

THE INDIGENOUS MOVEMENT

". . . as the peoples and nations of the world have come to recognize the existence and rights of those peoples who make up the Third World, the day must come, and will come, when the nations of the Fourth World will come to be recognized and respected . . ." The Dene Declaration, 1975

There are over 1000 indigenous organisations worldwide – most of them established in the last 20 years (see pp. 178-9). The forces of change – political, social, economic, and global have lent impetus to this new movement. Politically, one of the most important spurs has been decolonization in Africa, Asia, and the Caribbean. As the European powers withdrew – sometimes following negotiations, sometimes after bloody confrontation – and more than a hundred new states were formed, international relations transformed and opened up new opportunities, as well as conflicts. New international laws, too, offer a legal and moral framework for indigenous peoples. The right to self-determination is now enshrined in two covenants of the United Nations. And there are international laws on genocide and racial discrimination. But why limit the right to self-determination to the Third World? Why should it not also include indigenous peoples?

Economically, conditions have changed for those in the rich nations – Aotearoa (New Zealand), Australia, Canada, the Scandinavian countries – which have been at the forefront of the international movement. Although still among the poorest and most deprived in society, first peoples have won real improvements in health care, education, and welfare over the last 50 years. Populations are now growing rapidly. And governments who planned for native populations to disappear through assimilation are now forced to recognize the rise of independent, dynamic indigenous cultures.

The contemporary movement is a fusion (if sometimes a tense one) of traditional communities, angry at the renewed assault on their lands, and a

Treaties revisited Broken treaties have fuelled the indigenous peoples movement. Hundreds of agreements were signed in North America, Africa, Asia, and Oceania. Most were broken, some signed under duress, almost all were bedevilled by misunderstandings. The texts in the colonial language rarely tallied with the indigenous versions. And colonial concepts of sovereignty, land, and ownership had no equivalent in indigenous cultures. For first peoples, the question remains: do nation states see treaties as valid international agreements? To them, abiding by a treaty is a sacred duty for future generations. And since it is agreed between equal and independent states, a treaty is an acknowledgement of indigenous sovereignty. In 1989 the UN authorized a special study on treaties – an initiative that indigenous peoples hope will bring recognition of agreements.

National emblems *Dozens of indigenous nations now have their own flags. Some colours reflect the nature of their land. On the Aboriginal flag, (below) black represents the people, gold the sun, and red the blood spilt in defence of their land.*

The Treaty of Waitangi In the 1960s and 1970s Maori organizations demanded the return of lands lost subsequent to the signing of a treaty in 1840. The treaty guaranteed the Maori *"full, exclusive and undisturbed possession of their lands and estates, forests, fisheries and other properties"*, in exchange for the British Queen's right to buy land if the owner consented. In fact, the text was deliberately changed by the colonizers. It was a signal for a massive transfer of land from Maori to Crown ownership. From a land base totalling 25 million hectares prior to colonization, Maori territory has been reduced to only 1.6 million hectares.

Tent embassies *Aborigine supporters (above) demonstrate outside the Tent embassy set up in the grounds of Parliament House, Canberra, in 1972. In 1975 Maori organisations set up a tent embassy outside Parliament House in Auckland. As a result of this and further action, the government opened the Waitangi Tribunal in 1984 to examine land claims. Progress is slow, but the Waitangi Treaty is now a rallying cry for Maoris who seek self-government, the return of lands, and greater control over their affairs.*

new radical movement, frustrated with racism and their exclusion from the decision-making process. A new generation of indigenous leaders has emerged. Many activists are urban based – living away from their traditional communities – yet outsiders who face discrimination in society. Indigenous students set up many early organizations to counteract racism, especially in countries where large numbers of indigenous peoples live in cities. Some who lost their land migrated to the cities and suffered exploitation or unemployment have become active – the Mapuche of Santiago, for example. Others, including the Aymara in Bolivia learned the language of their colonizers, became professionals and entered mainstream political life.

AIMS, HOPES, DEMANDS

"We define our rights in terms of self-determination. We are not looking to dismember your States and you know it. But we do insist on the right to control our territory, our resources, the organization of our societies, our own decision-making institutions, and the maintenance of our own cultures and ways of life."
Geoff Clarke, National Coalition of Aboriginal Organizations of Australia addressing ILO, 1988

The key to survival for indigenous peoples is self-determination – the freedom to control their own lives. In the long term, first peoples want a secure land base held collectively by the community. They want to be treated as a "people", not as a simple numerical "population". And they want to manage their own affairs.

There is, however, a number of other basic rights that remain central to indigenous peoples' aspirations. They are asking for the right to set up their own schools and for their children to be taught in their own language. Peru is one of the few countries in the world officially to recognize two indigenous languages – Aymara and Quechua. Indigenous peoples also want the right to preserve their own sacred and archeological sites, their own

Consultation and consent Indigenous peoples are rarely consulted about development on their land. Decisions about a mining project, or settlement scheme may attract debate in political and financial circles. But those whose lives will be affected generally remain in the dark until the last minute. Now indigenous peoples want international protection. They want the right to be fully consulted. And above all, they want the right to say no.

Car scaffold burial *This piece of protest art makes a personal and a global statement. The sculptor's car – here enclosed in a funerary blanket and open to the elements in a Plains burial scaffold – was wrecked by a drunken driver. The insurance company refused to replace it. It was his only way to get to work, and his child had been born in it. The sculpture now stands as an effigy not only to the unrecognized struggles of indigenous peoples but to the incongruous priorities of modern life.*

Self determination First Peoples aspire to self-determination. They want to regain the right to develop their societies according to their own needs. Many had their own laws and legal systems long before colonizers introduced political frontiers and new laws. Demands for self-determination vary. A few peoples, such as the West Papuan and Kanaky peoples, want political independence. Others, including the Karen, Kachin, Shan, and other hill peoples of Burma, and the Igorots of the Philippines, are demanding autonomy within the state. Indigenous peoples in Canada and Aotearoa (New Zealand) want existing treaties honoured. Where they are a majority of the population, as in Bolivia, Peru, and Guatemala, they are fighting for democratic rights and full participation in national affairs. Self-determination is not restricted to narrow, political ends, it also includes control over local education, child care, health, and media.

Land A secure land base is vital to indigenous peoples. It is their means of economic survival. When indigenous peoples demand land rights, they include the resources beneath the soil, the trees and animals, the rivers, hills, coastal water, ice and air. Mother Earth incorporates all these elements. Indigenous peoples also speak of their collective and inalienable right to the land. Land, as they see it, is not a commodity to be bought and sold, but the collective responsibility of the community, which must be passed on to future generations. The land is more than just an economic resource, it is also the place where the spirits live, where their ancestors are buried, and where new generations will grow up. Separated from their land, indigenous peoples can become physically sick. Colonialism has broken the connection between many people and their traditional land. Now indigenous peoples are demanding protection of their lands. Some request the return of lost lands; others compensation. Above all, they are stating their need for sufficient land to survive.

art and sacred objects. Graves have been desecrated, the remains put on display and religious areas exploited for tourism. But there are signs of change. In Australia, Uluru (Ayers Rock), one of the most sacred sites, has been returned to Aboriginal ownership. And in some countries, museums are beginning to return the bones of ancestors.

First peoples are claiming the right to participate fully in the life of the nation state. The authority of elders, councils, and indigenous laws have often been limited since colonialism began. Maori and Aborigines have won some recognition of their customary legal practices. But few indigenous peoples are politically represented, even when they account for a large percentage of the national population, nor do they receive a fair share of the wealth. Powerful financial institutions, such as the World Bank, and transnational corporations have invested in damaging projects on indigenous lands (see pp. 74-133). First peoples are demanding that states impose stricter controls over their investments, that indigenous owners participate fully in future projects, and that native inhabitants and environments are protected by international regulations. Following pressure by human rights and environmental organizations, the World Bank has prepared guidelines for their own investments in indigenous areas. In certain cases the Bank has temporarily withdrawn funding.

Peace, sustainable development and a healthy, safe environment are priorities for all indigenous peoples, who are particularly affected by militarization and environmental degradation. They know they can offer specialist knowledge, and they want to play a central part in the discussions of the new generation. Their aim is not a Utopian dream nor a regression to a world free from development and technology. What they are asking for is to be consulted and to control decisions that affect not only their own survival but that of the environment and of all humankind. This might be assured if it is written into binding international agreements.

Stars and stripes
Native North Americans do not find their distinct nations are recognized. Instead their identity is imprisoned within the alien cultural and political values of the State.

Speeches

"From whence does authority flow? Who first established the principles of peace and freedom? Does it flow from the great assembly of the United Nations? That cannot be because these principles were here even before them. It seems to us that from the earliest times, man's natural state was to be free as our grandfathers told us. We believe that freedom is inherent to life. We recognize this principle as the key to peace and respect for one another, and the understanding of the natural law that prevails over all the universe and adherence to these laws is the only salvation of our future on the planet, Mother Earth."
Haudenosaunee People to UN Working Group on Indigenous Populations 1987

"The protection of indigenous peoples' religious freedom – in our experience in North America and Australia – is inseparable from land rights." Russell Barsh, Four Directions Council to UN Commission on Human Rights, 1984

"We are saying we have the right to determine our own lives. This right derives from the fact that we were here first." Robert Andre, Red Arctic Press

"Our Nations have a natural and rightful place within the family of Nations of the World. Our political, legal, social and economic systems developed in accordance with the laws of the Creator since time immemorial and continue to this day." Union of British Columbia Chiefs to UN Working Group on Indigenous Populations, 1987

"For what is the use of having good international standards years from now, if we no longer exist? What is the reason for harvesting the grass when the horse is already dead?" Representative 8 Philippines' Indigenous Organization to UN Working Group on Indigenous Populations, 1987

"We hereby demand yet again recognition of our humanity and our land rights. Hear us, White Australia, we are the spirit of our land. Our name is humanity. Our aims are self-determination and justice. We will not be defeated. We are our history, we are our culture, we are our land. We are now." Declaration of the People of Musgrave Park, Australia, 1982

LOCAL ACTION

"We try to encourage people to develop appropriate technologies – to rediscover the traditional ways of doing things which work and which do not destroy the Earth or its people, and to create new technologies which will support the survival of peoples in the shadow of the tremendously destructive technologies." Akwesasne Notes, 1979

Self-determination begins on a local level as communities oppose government policies that are ineffective, even harmful. Over the last 20 years, indigenous peoples have begun to take the initiative in important areas.

They have revived their languages, established schools, and are re-educating the young in traditional practices (see pp. 146-7). *"Education is the bottom line to our survival"*, say the Mohawk, a recognition shared by all indigenous peoples concerned for their future. In Australia, Canada, Colombia, Mexico, India, Aotearoa (New Zealand), Argentina, Venezuela, USA, and USSR indigenous peoples have begun to teach their own languages, history, religion, social customs, traditions, songs, and art. The methods vary. Aboriginal elders show children sacred sites and teach them how to gather bush foods. In Mexico, a national association of bilingual indigenous teachers is promoting equal fluency in native languages and Spanish. But in all cases indigenous-run schools form an integral part of the community.

Many groups have set up their own welfare systems, often combining modern medicine with traditional shamanistic practices and advising on AIDS, alcoholism, and drug abuse (see pp. 154-5). Communications between indigenous groups has grown in the last ten years. Television and radio stations, magazines, theatre, music, and art groups have helped to spread information, to promote discussion of vital issues as well as to reinforce cultural identity (see pp. 148-9). There are now, for example, over 400 periodicals by and about

New networks *Communication between indigenous groups has increased dramatically during the 1980s as technology has become cheaper and more readily available. Two-way, solar-powered radio, for example, allows an Aborigine to co-ordinate a local meeting (above). In North and South America, and particularly in Canada, dozens of new radio stations have emerged, and many are now demanding a share in national broadcasting services to broaden their audience.*

indigenous peoples worldwide. Networking, too, is growing. Many indigenous newspapers and centres now have micro-computers and electronic mail to extend their reach. Some individuals have set up successful businesses. And others who are becoming lawyers, doctors, teachers, politicians, and artists are trying to bridge the gap between indigenous and mainstream culture. Others are co-ordinating on a political level – to fight for appropriate development projects (see pp. 150-1), to manage resources (see pp. 152-3) and to campaign for self-determination.

SURVIVAL SCHOOLS
The Mohawks in Montreal

The movement to set up indigenous schools in the United States and Canada spread during the 1960s and 1970s, when indigenous peoples began to recognize that only through the re-education of their children could indigenous nations survive. The Kahnawake School is one of a number of survival schools, established and run by indigenous peoples.

The idea of a school for Montreal's Mohawk children began after a snowball fight between two boys in 1971. Both were guilty, but only one was suspended. The punished boy was Indian and the other was white. As a protest indigenous children at the school occupied the main auditorium for three days. They felt unwelcome in the school, they said. They had no Mohawk history or language lessons, and they faced daily discrimination. In a school of 2700 students only 400 or so were indigenous. The only Mohawk staffmember in the school was the janitor.

   The children were backed by their parents. They demanded accredited courses on Mohawk culture and indigenous teachers. Not only were indigenous peoples losing their identity in the national education system, they realized, but they were coming out of it with the lowest grades. A change was necessary. The parents won some concessions from the Quebec government; an Indian counsellor was appointed, some native teachers were recruited, and classes in Mohawk history and language were opened. But the people still felt unhappy. In 1978 they called a referendum to decide whether to create an Indian high school. There was overwhelming support from the community, but a firm "no" from the government. Once again the children and

their parents demonstrated, calling for assistance from their community. Teachers volunteered to work for nothing, while community leaders and local people found equipment and space. On 9 September 1978, after only four days, the Mohawk community had set up its own Indian-run school in Canada; the Kahnawake Survival School. *"Educating our own children is the bottom line to our survival, which we hold to be the most important and urgent priority before us."* Rokwaho, for the Mohawk Council of Chiefs of Akwesasne

Giving thanks *At the start of each day at Akwesasne Freedom School a student leads the children in thanking the many elements of creation (above): the trees, animals, wind, water, Earth, elders, spiritual messengers, medicines, birds, and the Creator.*

Traditional sports *Students are encouraged to take part in winter recreations such as cross-country skiing, ice skating, and snowshoeing (far left). Snowshoes are used for hunting, trapping, and living off the land in winter.*

Mohawk symbols *Students in traditional deerhide dresses (left), about to perform dances at a school festivity. They stand before an eagle, which signifies power, pride, and clear vision, and the tree of life, indicating growth and strength.*

HARNESSING TECHNOLOGY
Local radio for the Shuar

Local indigenous communities are now taking advantage of sophisticated technology: the Canadian Cree run an airline, the Cordillera peoples of the Philippines are managing their own development projects, Aborigines in Australia transmit television programmes in their languages, and the Blackfoot Indians in the USA have founded the first indigenous bank. By steering their own development, indigenous people can reap the benefits of innovation.

A schools radio programme, launched by the Shuar Indians of Ecuador in 1972, uses technology to serve their educational needs. Between 7.30 am and 1.30 pm every day a schools programme is broadcast to about 240 Shuar centres throughout Amazonian Ecuador. Shuar children listen to broadcasts in both Spanish and Shuar languages, using portable receivers. General education programmes and lessons in their own history and culture are accompanied by textbooks written by the Shuar themselves. Programmes of general interest follow the schools programmes and these broadcasts have encouraged the formation of local associations.

Before the advent of local radio, schooling was available only in government-run boarding schools. Far from their community, Shuar children were taught in a predominantly non-indigenous class, and parents were hard pressed to afford the maintenance costs of the schools. This, combined with inflexible regimes, led to low academic performance and a high drop-out rate. The radio school has transformed the children's performance, and at the same time halved the cost of their education.

Local impact *Shuar radio transmissions reach as far as neighbouring Indian communities, the Secoya and the Waorani, providing a focus for civil and land rights issues.*

Shuar schools *Shuar children benefit from local broadcasts in a school run by a Catholic mission. The radio service has enabled children to return to their villages from the government-run schools.*

THE POWER OF THE BODONG
The Cordillera Peoples' Alliance

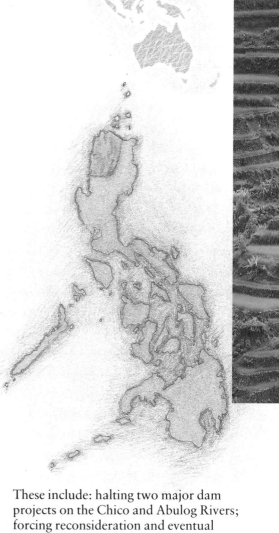

The Cordillera region of the Philippines, home to three-quarters of a million indigenous Igorots, contains abundant natural wealth. But exploitation of these resources has brought riches to outsiders and impoverishment to the people. Severe threats presented by dams and logging operations have been met by resistance organized through traditional structures.

Traditionally the "bodong" is a peace pact between two powerful individuals representing neighbouring but fiercely independent communities. It provides a mechanism for the resolution of inter-community conflict short of bloody feuding. The "new" anti-dam bodong united all communities into one pact against the larger external threats.

In the 1970s, the Marcos dictatorship used the army to try to implement an internationally financed exploitation of Cordillera resources. At the heart of the programme was a plan funded by the World Bank to construct four dams in the Chico valley – home to 85,000 Igorots. The dams would have submerged villages, graves, rice terraces, and orchards, and destroyed Chico valley culture.

Resistance organized through the bodong spread along the valley. Fierce military repression failed because the worse abuses became, the stronger grew the unity and determination of the peoples involved in the bodong.

In 1984 the Cordillera Peoples' Alliance (CPA) was formed as a federation of indigenous organizations. Many of the CPAs present, 130 member organizations, including the original Cordillera Bodong Association, are based on indigenous structures and processes. The Cordillera peoples have achieved great successes.

These include: halting two major dam projects on the Chico and Abulog Rivers; forcing reconsideration and eventual withdrawal of World Bank and Japanese government funding; closing a logging and pulp production project; and blocking other timber and mining companies. Today they have their own regional development strategy based on self-reliance and sustainability.

From the programme of the Cordillera Peoples' Alliance

○   The indigenous peoples of the Cordillera should be given perpetual and inalienable collective rights to their ancestral lands.

○   The Constitution of the Philippines should recognize the autonomous region of the Cordillera within a democratic state.

○   Igorot people should have the right to the disposition, use, and management of the natural resources on their ancestral domain.

○   Decisions of importance should be taken by the self-governing institutions of the Cordillera peoples.

○   The Cordillera peoples should have control over their own culture; and commercial exploitation, especially by tourism, should be combatted.

○   In view of the poverty of the Cordillera, increased state resources should be made available for regional development.

Link with the ancestors *The Igorot terrace builders regard their fields (above), constructed over generations, as a priceless inheritance held in trust for future generations.*

Protest *Igorot tribespeople (right) demonstrate against the construction of dams on the Chico River. The World Bank's plan was to provide cheap power to attract foreign investment to the adjacent lowlands.*

FISHING RIGHTS, USA
The treaty tribes of the Pacific Northwest

In many parts of the world today tribal groups are excluded from making decisions about the important natural resources upon which they have traditionally depended. Governments often fail to recognize indigenous peoples' resource rights or management capabilities. As a result, resource users often cannot harvest their fair share, and they have no say in how resources are used and regulated. In contrast, the treaty tribes of the American Northwest, after a century of struggle to regain rights guaranteed in the 1850s, have had their rights affirmed in court and implemented in practice. Today 20 treaty tribes of western Washington and four on the Columbia River are full participants in resource management.

In the Northwest fish have been the centre of the economy and way of life for centuries. Under treaties agreed during the 1850s the tribes were guaranteed exclusive rights to fish on their reservation, and held a right "in common with" other citizens in the off-reservation fishing places. Over the century that followed, several factors severely restricted their off-reservation fishery: the growth of the non-Indian commercial and sports fishing, state restrictions, and environmental destruction of the fish habitat. After many years of struggling against these obstacles, Indians engaged in "fish-ins", fishing in defiance of state law, but in accordance with Indian interpretations of the treaties. The protests led to court cases. The pivotal case was in 1974, when it was ruled that "in common with" meant sharing equally: the tribes had the right to catch 50 per cent of the harvestable fish destined for their traditional fishing places. Further, the decision recognized tribal authority to

Fishing techniques *A technician feeds young salmon at an Indian hatchery (above right), where modern equipment, sophisticated research programmes, and computer technology are employed to gain maximum yields.*

Leaping silver salmon *(above) by Andy Fernando and Brenda Snyder, is the logo of an Indian fish-packaging company.*

manage their fishing in the traditional places. Five years of controversy followed.

In 1979 the US Supreme Court affirmed the ruling. Federal legislation and funding for a new fishery enhancement and management programme followed. Over the last decade a co-operative fisheries management system has evolved, including a variety of mechanisms for the co-ordination and resolution of disputes between the various parties.

For the tribes it has been a protracted, difficult path from the treaty grounds to the courtrooms and now to the conference rooms, where the important decisions about Northwest fisheries management are made. In the process a traditional way of making a livelihood has been restored.

"We cannot let the confrontation of the past dictate the shape of the future. Government to government, we can work together toward a better tomorrow." Bill Frank Jr., Nisqually Indian

OUR WELFARE
Aborigine self-determination

Until recently the official policy toward Aborigines was that the authorities knew best. That paternalistic period is now on the wain. *"Self-management and self-sufficiency are the basic concepts of modern Australian policy approaches to its indigenous peoples"*, claims the government. Aborigines for their part are no longer willing to accept state-run welfare programmes.

The changes began in the 1970s, when it became clear that government policy was not working. Aborigines were still disadvantaged, badly housed, unemployed, ill-educated, and in poor health. The problem was not money, since the government had substantially increased its expenditure on welfare programmes during the previous decade. The problem was attitude: the state, mainly through its white civil servants, was controlling how funds were spent. Aborigines were treated as dependent children.

It was then that Aborigines began setting up their own programmes. They formed health services to tackle the serious difficulties in remote communities and deprived inner cities; legal services to represent Aborigines in court; Aboriginal child welfare schemes and schools. For the first time disadvantaged Aborigines could receive help from their own people.

The government has backed the move toward greater Aboriginal control over resources. Aborigines were appointed to the senior posts in the Department of Aboriginal Affairs. An Aboriginal Development Commission – with an all-Aboriginal board of directors – receives over US$80 million annually for housing, low-cost loans, and enterprise schemes. There are now some 2000 Aboriginal organizations benefiting from government

Aboriginal health worker training programme *In central Australia, Aboriginal technicians (right) are being trained to look after their own people on a programme that acknowledges the importance of both Western and indigenous medicine.*

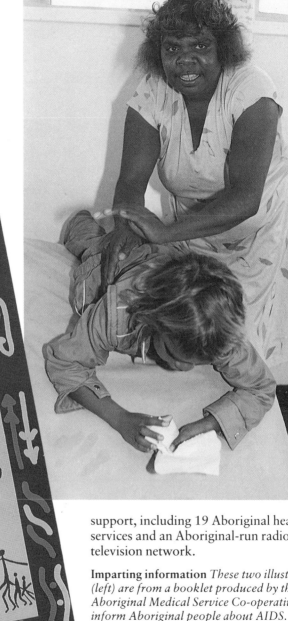

support, including 19 Aboriginal health services and an Aboriginal-run radio and television network.

Imparting information *These two illustrations (left) are from a booklet produced by the Aboriginal Medical Service Co-operative to inform Aboriginal people about AIDS.* "ABORIGINAL PEOPLE. Protect yourself from getting AIDS and you will be protecting your race and your culture."

GOVERNMENT REACTIONS

"We declare that all laws, rules, regulations, orders-in-council and acts passed on or enacted by you, and your federal, provincial and territorial governments, which interfere with our sovereignty, must be re-examined in the light of our position. The right to make laws which govern our people must be returned to our people." Declaration by the Ojibway-Cree Nation, 1977

Pressures are now on governments to grant indigenous peoples control over their land, resources, and development projects affecting them. Some have taken measures to enhance self-management and regional autonomy. Australia, Nicaragua, and the Philippines, for example, now acknowledge the need for some form of indigenous self-determination. And The James Bay Treaty between Cree, Inuit, and the Quebec government has established formal structures for local self-management.

Some new economic deals have also been struck. The Inuit have secured large areas of their original territory in northern Canada, and over 17.8 million hectares in Alaska, as well as legal incentives to establish businesses. The Waitangi Tribunal of Aotearoa (New Zealand) is now considering Maori land claims. In Peru the 1974 Law of Native Communities Act began the process of titling land. But such tentative acts are yet to take full effect in many cases. In Peru, despite legislation, most indigenous communities do not have legal title. In Alaska, traditional communities fear they may lose control over their land and resources in 1991 when outsiders will have the right to buy stock in native companies. Political measures are also being taken. In Nicaragua, there is a regional autonomy plan, which includes 100,000 Miskito, Rama, and Sumu peoples. Two directly-elected governments will have a large measure of control over natural resources, education and local taxation, and indigenous languages will be officially recognized for the first

From rights to wrongs A year after Cory Aquino's government was elected in the Philippines in 1986, it introduced a new constitution. It promised to create autonomous regions and to protect the right of indigenous peoples to their ancestral lands, and initiated health, education, and social projects. But the state is negotiating with the EEC to initiate a large development programme on the land of the Cordillera peoples, without consulting indigenous organizations. And clauses providing for reparation of damage and indigenous control over future extractions have also been cut from the draft autonomy text. The final version will be put to a referendum.

Inviting advice *The Saami of Scandinavia and USSR, are subject to four different legal systems, even though they are one people. In 1956 the Saami peoples of Finland, Norway, and Sweden formed the Nordic Saami Council, to represent their common aspirations – to protect their lands, language, culture, and organizations. In response, the Nordic governments have set up bodies with a limited advisory role, such as the Ministerial Working Group for Saami Affairs in Sweden, and the Norwegan Saami Council. A Saami "Parliament" was elected in Finland in 1972, in Norway in 1989, and Sweden is now considering following suit. The Saami are not demanding separate statehood, but a set of common standards for each country.*

time. In 1987, Australian Prime Minister Bob Hawke announced a forthcoming treaty that would recognize Aborigines as the original owners of Australia, and provide a basis for compensation. However, although Aborigines have title to 12 per cent of the Australian land mass, their holdings are mainly in the desert and rugged uplands of two states. In the five other states, they own less than 1 per cent of the land.

Many territories are facing growing criticism. Government agencies set up to protect and promote indigenous rights, have, on occasion, acted against the interests of indigenous peoples. Brazil's National Indian Foundation (FUNAI), for example, is negotiating access to indigenous lands, instead of guarding them against exploitation. In India, positive discrimination is written into the constitution, seats are reserved in both national and state parliaments and most public services have a quota for indigenous peoples. Yet tribal peoples remain the poorest group in Indian society.

Despite these reservations, there is room for cautious optimism in many parts of the world.

THE INTERNATIONAL ARENA

"Governments come and go, but the peoples of the world remain a permanent constituency of the United Nations." (Temporary) President of Uganda, 1979

Co-ordinated local action is lending force to the growing international movement. Those separated by political boundaries are developing links and presenting common programmes to their respective governments. Community-based and national groups, frustrated by the broken promises or indifference of governments have been forced to seek international support. The international arena, and, particularly, the United Nations has thus become the focus of political activity.

A common strategy is emerging – a campaign to get the UN to proclaim a Declaration of Indigenous Rights. This would affirm first peoples' rights to self-determination, to their land, and to their culture. It would serve as a moral incentive to governments to return them control over their lives and futures.

International organizations, particularly the International Labour Organisation (ILO) and the UN Commission on Human Rights have developed a growing concern for indigenous peoples. They have, for example, examined allegations of slavery in Paraguay, ethnocide in Brazil, and genocide in Guatemala and the Philippines. In the last ten years they have taken important initiatives. The UN has established a special working group to help draft an indigenous declaration. In addition to five expert members, one from each geopolitical region, there are several hundred representatives from governments and indigenous groups – with equal speaking rights. Meanwhile the ILO, which has the only binding international law for indigenous peoples (revised in 1989), has looked into many problems. It sent a mission to investigate abuses against the 600,000 tribespeople of the Chittagong Hill Tracts in Bangladesh. The government then took measures to grant some local autonomy and guarantee land ownership. Only time will tell whether these steps lead to real improvements.

Aiming for the General Assembly Indigenous peoples are not directly represented at the United Nations General Assembly. Representatives from recognized indigenous organizations, however, can speak for a limited time at the Commission on Human Rights (below), which takes place in Geneva in February and March. Its recommendations are discussed by the General Assembly in its meeting from September to December. In 1982, the Commission agreed to an annual Working Group on Indigenous Populations, where indigenous peoples can meet to recommend future legislation to protect their rights .

"All peoples have the right to self-determination. By virtue of that right they freely determine their political status and freely pursue their economic, social and cultural development." Article 1 of the International Covenants on Economic, Social and Cultural Rights and on Civil and Political Rights.

A foot in two worlds *Many indigenous peoples are responding to the challenge to adapt to the bureaucracy of national and international systems, while maintaining their integrity. A Xavante leader (left) approaches a meeting with government officials carrying both briefcase and traditional war club.*

NON GOVERNMENTAL ORGANIZATIONS

INTERNATIONAL SUPPORT
Peruvian Indian route to the UN

Faced with increasing assaults on their land and its resources, Amazonian Indian communities are achieving representation at international level. To this end, people such as the Amarakaeri of Peru have now formed links with all indigenous peoples in Peru and the Amazon Basin.

Every evening Amarakaeri leaders chat informally to each family group. This is not idle talk. They are sounding the opinions of the villagers, giving the whole village a voice in decision making. More formal meetings take place every few months for outside matters, such as exploitation by foreigners and land incursions.

Since 1982 an organization known as FENAMAD, the Federation of Native Communities of the Madre de Dios region of Peru, has represented indigenous communities on questions of land titles, health, and education. Representatives from the Amarakaeri attend FENAMAD meetings. Now all five Amarakaeri communities own recognized land titles and more than 18 pupils have entered secondary or tertiary education.

FENAMAD is also represented at AIDESEP, which represents indigenous peoples of the Peruvian Amazon. The AIDESEP magazine, *Voz Indigena*, provides a communication channel for all indigenous Peruvian organizations.

AIDESEP and an Amazonian Indian umbrella organization, COICA, regularly attend the UN Working Group on Indigenous Populations. Formed in 1984, COICA is a confederation of indigenous organizations of Bolivia, Brazil, Colombia, Ecuador, Peru, Surinam, and Venezuela.

In 1987 a statement to the UN by COICA made special reference to gold miners invading Amarakaeri communities, which the Amarakaeri would have had no voice to deal with on their own.

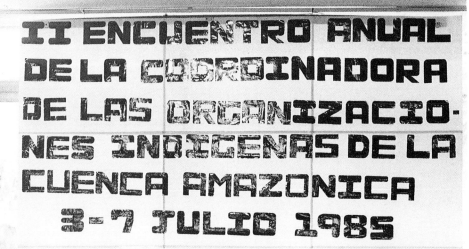

II ENCUENTRO ANUAL DE LA COORDINADORA DE LAS ORGANIZACIO-NES INDIGENAS DE LA CUENCA AMAZONICA 3-7 JULIO 1985 SEDE LIMA - PERU

Village voices *Indigenous South American organizations meet at the annual COICA conference (see text, left). All delegates to the meetings are from grass roots organizations: the interests of Amarakaeri from the San Jose del Karene region of Peru are represented by FENAMAD and AIDESEP. Through COICA, the Amarakaeri, and all indigenous peoples of the Amazon, have a voice at the United Nations.*

COALITIONS

"Until recently we didn't have much reason to think that the white man would ever understand, in fact want to understand, the Indians, our ways of thinking and living . . . It is true, though, that recently we have seen groups of Indians and white people working together and organizing in order to try and change the way people think." Paulinho Paiakan, Kayapo chief

Indigenous peoples are now looking beyond their own individual struggles. They have defined a shared agenda and are pursuing their common goals in unison. At the same time, their demands are reaching an increasingly sympathetic audience among all those concerned for the future.

The survival of first peoples rests on a radical change in political and economic conditions. Demands for self-determination and land are a direct challenge to the authority of governments, and can translate into local political conflict. International support is therefore crucial.

Since the 1960s a wave of pro-indigenous organizations has emerged to join well-established bodies, such as the Anti-Slavery Society. Survival International in the UK, the Copenhagen-based International Work Group for Indigenous Affairs, Cultural Survival in the USA, Gesellschaft für bedrohte Völker in Germany, the Dutch Workgroup for Indigenous Peoples, the Swiss group Incomindios and other smaller groups are actively campaigning, publishing and raising funds for indigenous peoples. Human rights organizations, such as Amnesty International, are also increasingly concerned with indigenous rights.

On a broader level, the aims of human rights organizations, environmental organizations, religious groups, development NGOs, scientists, and political parties are converging with those of first peoples. And together they now form a global network for human survival working to promote human rights and a healthy environment.

SURVIVAL INTERNATIONAL for the rights of threatened tribal peoples

Survival International   310 Edgware Road

Human interests *Support from popular movements and human rights organizations (right) is crucial to indigenous peoples. The support can also be mutual. Environmental organizations, such as Friends of the Earth, now recognize that the world's wildernesses can only survive with the help of their native inhabitants, and campaign for indigenous rights, while drawing on the peoples' knowledge of their environment.*

THE SORT OF BANGLES KIDS WEAR IN THAILAND.

The slave-market in Bangkok is just around the corner from the railway station. Children, some just 6 or 7 years old, are sold for about £250.

Each comes with a written receipt.

Most end up in back-street sweat shops. Some are chained in cellars, packing opium into pellets. Others make fluorescent lights. They have to bite through electric flex with their teeth.

Beating, cutting and scalding is common.

If a girl is pretty, she'll escape these horrors. She'll be sold into prostitution.

In Bangladesh, child prostitutes of 7 and upwards work from 8 in the morning till midnight.

A madame buys the girls for £80 or £90 each.

To get the most from her investment she'll punish slackers by beating them and hanging them by their hands.

Some girls are smuggled across the border into India, where slave-traders sell them for £240 each.

If a girl has fair skin, her price can double.

In India, young boys are sold into slavery to work in carpet factories.

If the loom-masters run out of boys to buy, they kidnap them.

Often the boys are just 5 or 6 years old. With their small, nimble fingers, children are just right for the job. They can knot the carpet-thread faster.

They're ill-fed and they work a 10-hour ...

If they try to run away, they're slung up ... down from a tree and branded.

If they cry, they're beaten with stones in a cloth.

In Yugoslavia, gypsy children are boug ... £100 and smuggled across the hills into I ...

Some are just 8 years old.

They're taken in the boots of cars t ... outside Milan and Turin. Then they st ... training. They become experts at snatch ... picking pockets and breaking into houses.

The children are then sold again, this time to criminal gangs. The price is £12,000 each.

They can't escape. The children depend on their new masters for food, shelter and clothing.

If they don't bring in a good haul each day, they're beaten.

In Pakistan, children are kidnapped and put into work-camps. During the day they're made to work in stone quarries and on road-building.

They're chained up at night.

If they try to escape, they're shot dead.

You probably thought that slavery was abolished in eighteen something or other.

Tragically, it's thriving. The Anti-Slavery Society is as overworked now as when it was set up in 1839.

today because ...

This ad won't run again. It's our one chan ... to raise some cash to take us into our 150th year. Please help.

THE ANTI SLAVERY SOCIETY.

DIPLOMACY AND DIRECTNESS
Kayapo halt the Altamira Dam

Brazil aims to quadruple its electricity supply in the next 25 years to meet the needs of mining companies and cities. Plans to build 136 dams, 68 of them on indigenous land, were opposed by the indigenous population. But the Kayapo Indians began a well-planned publicity programme to rally opinion and halt the building of five local dams.

The dam-building programme could inundate up to 250,000sq km (97,000 sq miles) and displace 500,000 people. It is not only a potential human disaster but could also be working against the long-term economic and environmental interests of Brazil.

In 1988 a group of Kayapo Indians launched an extraordinary campaign to halt the construction of the Barbaquara and Kararao dams, which threatened their territory at Altamira on the Xingu River. Their leaders visited the headquarters of the World Bank to request the withdrawal of a US$500 million loan. They met US senators, toured European capitals, talked to members of parliament, and explained their concerns to environmentalists and human rights groups. Then, in February 1989, at the site of the proposed dam, the Indians convened an international meeting. The fate of the Altamira dam had become international news.

In March, following the pressure, the World Bank announced that it would no longer fund the dam. Instead it is ready to support improvements in electricity transmission and distribution. The result is more than just a victory for the Kayapo. It has challenged the economic strategy of the Brazilian government.

"We don't need your electricity. Electricity won't give us food. . . . We need our forests to hunt and gather in. We don't want your dam. Everything you tell us is a lie."
Kayapo woman to Brazilian official at Altamira meeting

Press conference *About 650 Indians from 40 tribes met at the site of the proposed dam. Nearly 400 journalists and representatives from non-governmental organizations attended. The Brazilian Electronorte promised compensation; an apparently empty promise.*

PELA VIDA DO
BARRAGEM CIM

On record *A Kayapo leader at the Altamira meeting discusses video coverage with another Indian. Indigenous people see the value of mastering technology. Videos on forest destruction are being made by Indians for distribution to the press and to their supporters.*

A GLOBAL VOICE

"We are on the one hand the most oppressed people on the globe. On the other hand, we are the hope for the future of people on the planet. The peoples that surround us now are beginning to experience in the 20th century that there are limitations to the kinds of economic organization that define their societies." John Mohawk, Haudenosaunee writer

Indigenous peoples are one of the world's most persistent voices of conscience, alerting humankind to the dangers of environmental destruction. And as the world searches for alternative strategies to deal with global problems, it is turning more and more to indigenous peoples. Much of their respect for nature, their methods of resource management, social organization, values, and culture are finding echoes in the writing of scientists, philosophers, politicians, and thinkers.

In the face of an increasingly unsustainable world economy, ever-faster rates of productivity, consumption, and change, respect is growing for ways of life attuned to the constraints of natural environments. Ranged on the frontline of the ecological crisis, indigenous peoples have been forced to defend their culture, lands, and way of life. They have developed new strategies to protect the environment, to manage declining resources, and to advance the cause of peace. With financial support the Kuna Indians of Panama have established and fully manage a forest park and botanical reserve on their territory. The Inuit have initiated an Arctic Conservation Programme. Indigenous women in the USA have formed a network that campaigns creatively for social change. Pacific islanders – and particularly women – are working for a nuclear-free Pacific. All are fighting to ensure a future for their own children and in so doing are working for all humankind.

"We must go beyond the arrogance of human rights. We must go beyond the ignorance of civil rights. We must step into the reality of natural rights because all the natural world has a right to existence. We are only a small part of it. There can be no trade off." John Trudell at the Survival Gathering, 1980

Sustainable livelihoods, as in Tibet (above) are crucial to the preservation of the environment.

". . . to harm the Earth is to heap contempt on its creator. The whites too shall pass – perhaps sooner than other tribes. Continue to contaminate your bed, and you will one night suffocate in your own waste. When the buffalo are all slaughtered, the wild horses all tamed, the secret corners of the forest heavy with the scent of many men, and the view of the ripe hills blotted by talking wires, where is the thicket? Gone? Where is the eagle? Gone. And what is it to say goodbye to the swift and the hunt, the end of living and the beginning of survival." Californian Indian

"We see it like this: it is as if we are all in a canoe travelling through time. If someone begins to make a fire in their part of the canoe, and another begins to pour water inside the canoe, or another begins to piss in the canoe, it will affect us all. And it is the responsibility of each person in the canoe to ensure that it is not destroyed. Our planet is like one big canoe travelling through time. The destruction of the forest is everyone's concern." Ailton Krenak, Brazilian Union of Indian Nations (UNI)

NUCLEAR REACTIONS
Building peace in the Pacific

The Pacific islanders are protesting, in order to survive as a people. The Nuclear-Free and Independent Pacific movement is an indigenous organization working toward building a nuclear-free Pacific. It is also a protest against the colonial domination that introduced the nuclear threat and, with it, the ecological destruction of the Pacific islands.

The movement began in Fiji in 1975, by adopting a People's Charter for a Nuclear-Free Pacific. It was a response to the nuclear presence of the US, USSR, French and British governments, turning the Pacific into the most nuclearized region in the world (see page pp. 114-5). On the island of Belau in 1980, a group of women insisted on the world's first anti-nuclear constitution against strong opposition from the USA.

Protest action has also been used to advance the nuclear-free cause. In 1982, the Kwajalein Islanders were forced to move to Ebeye Island, a ghetto colony, because of the damage done by the US long-range missile tests fired into the atoll. They protested with a series of "sail-ins", called "Operation Homecoming", to re-occupy their land, in defiance of the US armed forces.

But freedom from nuclear weapons requires independence from outside powers. In 1983, in an attempt to achieve this, the People's Charter incorporated into its aims the withdrawal of all colonial powers from the area.

The nuclear-free movement has united nearly all the Pacific islands. Its aim of making the Pacific a nuclear-free zone has been adopted by trade unions and church groups. The South Pacific Forum, a regional forum of 13 Pacific states, has

Fighting for independence *Charlie Ching from the Tahitian Independence Party burns a French flag outside the French consulate in Auckland, Aotearoa (New Zealand). Tahiti, in French Polynesia, has been affected by atmospheric and underground tests carried out by the French government.*

Majuro Island, in the Marshall Islands, has escaped US missile testing.

also adopted part of the movement's programme. In 1985 the Forum negotiated the Treaty of Rarotonga, which prohibits the ownership, use, stationing and testing of nuclear weapons and the sea-dumping of nuclear waste. Eight states have already signed the treaty, and so has China. The USSR has signed two of the protocols, but the UK, USA, and France have yet to sign.

"We are only small – very few thousand people out there on tiny islands, but we are doing our part to stop this nuclear madness. And although we are few we have done it. Which means you can do it too."
Darlene Leju-Johnson, Marshall Islander

BEST OF BOTH WORLDS
The Matsigenka of Peru

Indigenous people who have maintained traditional agricultural methods and who are secure on their land are in a strong position to develop small areas for cash crops. This raises their standard of living, contributes to the national economy, and even improves their bargaining power.

Cultural Survival, a human rights group in the USA, has helped set up direct sales of local nuts by Amazonian Indians to a US ice-cream manufacturer. Bodyshop, a British-based chain of shops, is researching how forest produce suitable for skin care can be bought directly from indigenous peoples.

In Peru, the Matsigenka of the Upper Urubamba River have developed a judicious mix of commercial and subsistence agriculture: 40 of their 3200 hectares of land are under coffee and cacao cultivation, intercropped with their own foods. A secure land base has helped them to control their own development and prevent colonization by outsiders.

Self-sufficiency has allowed the community to minimize its dependence on the market economy. The 300 to 600kg (150 to 300lbs) of coffee produced annually brings in only up to US$300, but it is sufficient to buy goods unobtainable locally. The indigenous community enjoys a higher level of nutrition and better conditions of health than those among the colonists.

In the last 30 years, the areas surrounding the Matsigenka territory have been planted by colonists with coffee and other commercial crops. But commodity prices fluctuate and good years do not always succeed each other. Recently the market price of coffee dropped by 50 per cent. A dramatic cut in income inevitably means a drop in living standards and nutrition, as all foods are imported at high cost into the area.

Without any forest to hunt in or any land set aside for domestic food production, colonists face a grimmer future than the Matsigenka who have learned to get the best of both worlds.

Cushma weaving *Matsigenka women weave long garments known as cushmas. These may be sold or exchanged for axes, machetes, clothes, salt, hammocks and food unobtainable locally. But coffee produces the cash to buy most of these trade goods.*

Matsigenka village *Clearings are on territory which is secured by a land title. This secure base has helped the Matsigenka control their own development and prevent colonization by outsiders. It has enabled them to establish permanent coffee plantations that produce enough income to buy goods from outside.*

STRENGTH TO STRENGTH
Women carve their future

Women are the bearers of tradition, and as such they are the key to continuity in indigenous societies. But as first peoples are forced to adapt to modern development, to the destruction of the environment and their traditional lands, the role of women within indigenous societies is changing. They are now uniting to protest against injustices, to improve services, and to take control over their land.

Many of the women left widowed in Guatemala – indirect victims of military injustice against indigenous peoples – were left without support and with insufficient food. International assistance was forthcoming after organized protests in 1989 by 8000 widows, but was pocketed by corrupt officials so that little reached the women. Their protests led to imprisonment and beatings by the police. But the women, united by their determination to be able to bring up their children, are fighting back.

In India, education is helping a new generation of Santal women to win the attention of the government. By building local schools they are carving their own future and gaining recognition for their mother tongue and script.

The Indigenous Women's Network was established in 1984 to help co-ordinate the struggles of women in different countries. The network is supported by women from America and the Pacific, and represents the young and old, urban and rural. Their meetings address such issues as traditional families, domestic abuse, legal defence, natural resource management, and environmental protection.

The first International Indigenous Women's Conference took place in Adelaide, Australia, in July 1989, attended by 1500 women, from 15 countries. In a "Declaration of Unity", the women

MADRE DEL MUNDO
ARTIST MARSHA A. GOMEZ
MOTHER'S DAY
PEACE ACTION
1988

Women's Power *Bontoc women from the Cordillera of the Philippines (above) have started a movement known as "Women's Power". After successfully stopping the counting of votes in a rigged election in 1988 they have worked locally to improve education, health, and control over their land.*

Madre del Mundo *This life-size sculpture (left) by Texan artist and activist, Marsha Gomez, sits facing the Missile Test Site in the Nevada desert. It is a gesture of peace by an American group of artists, Artistas Indigenas, who promote the social and political roles of women through their art.*

affirmed their *"solidarity with one another and the land our mother, who through generations has witnessed our struggles drenched in blood"*. Some of the participants were traditional Aboriginal women who had broken with custom to attend the meeting by leaving their husbands in charge of the children.

We have worked to change education, health, environment and institutions for the betterment of our people. As indigenous women, we have personally struggled against overpowering forces. . . . Statement by the Indigenous Women's Network, 1984

ENVIRONMENT AND THE ECONOMY
Inuit survival strategy

The culture and identity of the Inuit people depend on their ability to harvest the wildlife of the region and to conserve the ecosystem. Faced with oil and gas extraction, and now the latest news that their Arctic homeland behaves like a global accumulator of pollutants from other areas of the world, the Inuit have developed a conservation strategy that encompasses both their environmental defence and economic development.

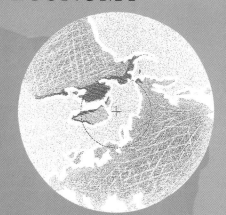

Inuit people from Alaska, Canada, Greenland, and USSR (see pp. 28-9) are represented at the Inuit Circumpolar Conference. The ICC has developed plans to protect 6.5 million sq km (2.5 million sq miles) of vulnerable Arctic environment, provide for Inuit subsistence needs, and maintain the productivity and the biological diversity of the Inuit homeland, thereby forming a basis for sustainable economic development. Known as the Inuit Regional Conservation Strategy (IRCS), these plans draw on indigenous culture, skills and values but also take into account scientific knowledge of the area.

In 1980 a World Conservation Strategy was launched, developed by the United Nations Environment Programme, the Food and Agriculture Organization, UNESCO, the International Union for the Conservation of Nature and Natural Resources(IUCN) and the World Wide Fund for Nature. Conservation programmes have since been started in more than 40 countries. The Inuit Regional Conservation Strategy, launched in 1986, is part of the World Conservation Strategy: it is the world's first regional programme and the first developed by an indigenous people.

The IRCS has so far:-
○ Prepared a register of Inuit environmental experts
○ Written a manual of Inuit Resource Management
○ Set up a data base to provide environmental information
○ Designated protected areas for caribou and sites of cultural significance
○ Set up projects in communities based on sustainable use of resources
○ Spread information in and out of the area on sustainable development in the Arctic
○ Carried out research on management of shared resources
○ Worked for international representation

In June 1989, the ICC was given the prestigious Global 500 Award by the United Nations Environment Programme in recognition of its "environmental management of part of the Arctic circumpolar region".

Hunting expedition *Inuit from north Greenland hunt wildlife using dog sleds. A hunters' association in the Thule area prohibits the use of motorized transport in winter. Sleds can travel on thinner ice than skidoos, and move with more ease on the rough, ridged, "pressure ice". The use of dog sleds also helps maintain Inuit culture and identity as a distinct people.*

THE FUTURE

"It seems to us that from the earliest times, man's natural state was to be free as our grandfathers told us and we believe that freedom is inherent to life. We recognize this principle as the key to peace, respect for one another and the understanding of the natural law that prevails over all the universe and adherence to this law is the only salvation of our future on the planet, Mother Earth." Oren Lyons, Onondaga

"One thing we know. Our God is the same God. This earth is precious to Him. Even the white man cannot be exempt from the common destiny. We may be brothers after all. We shall see." Chief Seattle

"We need to start educating the West...teaching them some social alternatives which place priority on humankind – not profits, not political power, not bombs, but on humanity." John Mohawk

Predictions about the future are rarely more than guesswork – we are continously surprised by the turn of events. However, many now agree that our survival depends on more sustainable management of the Earth's resources, and greater international co-operation. At the same time, there is a growing desire to control affairs on a more human scale – to move away from hierarchies and centralization, and to rethink how we organize politically.

The experiences and values of indigenous peoples may well take on a special significance. Their struggle for self-determination is part of a larger struggle for freedom; their beliefs about nature offer insights into how the whole environment should be protected; their social organizations may throw into question our own fragmented communities.

Too often we think we are powerless to change events, or even to protest. Yet we need a common humanitarian culture, and those who suffer most need the support of those who are free to speak out. Alliances and concerned individuals do bring about change (see pp. 186-7 for addresses).

Indigenous peoples ask no more than the right to determine their own development and future. We all wish no less for ourselves. As a violent century draws to a close, it is time to listen to those saner voices which stretch back to the birth of human society.

"The concept of development in a developing country is not necessarily the same as that understood by one belonging to a "developed" country. In a developing country the idea of development is closely linked with the wish for freedom — freedom to run one's own affairs the way one knows and believes, based on familiar traditions and ways of life. Freedom is in fact development, whether material progress and wealth are realized to the extent expected or not." Francis Bugotu, Solomon Islands

INDIGENOUS ORGANIZATIONS

Very few peoples of the world live in total isolation from their neighbours. An increasing awareness by indigenous peoples of their social, political, and economic importance, and of their need for repre-

sentation, is reflected in the growing number of grass-roots organizations. This map can only show a small fraction of the many thousands of such organizations throughout the world, ranging from small village

Arctic and Europe
1. Inuit Circumpolar Conference (ICC)
2. Nordic Saami Council

Canada and North America
3. Dene Nation
4. Assembly of First Nations (AFN)
5. Metis National Council
6. Coalition of First Nations
7. Grand Councils of Treaty Areas; Grand Council of the Crees
8. Union of New Brunswick Indians
9. Four Directions Council
10. Indigenous Women's Network
11. Western Shoshone National Council
12. American Indian Movement (AIM)
13. National Indian Youth Council (NIYC)
14. Indian Law Resource Center
15. International Indian Treaty Council (IITC)
16. The Six Nation Confederacy (Haudenosaunee)

Central America
17. Alianza de Profesionales Indigenas Bilinguas (APIBAC)
18. FIPI UCIZONI
19. Congreso de Organizaciones Indios de Centroamerica, Mexico y Panama
20. Organizacion Indigena Nahuatl
21. Asociacion Nacional Indigena Salvadorena (ANIS)
22. Comite de Unidades Campesinas (CUC)
23. Toledo Maya Cultural Council
24. YATAMA
25. Consejo de Organizaciones Indigenas de Central America
26. Asociacion de Empleados Kuna (AEK)
27. Congreso Guaymi
28. Movimiento de la Juventud Kuna (MJK)

South America
29. Organizacion de las Naciones Indigenas de Colombia (ONIC)
30. Consejo Regional Indigena de Cauca (CRIC)
31. Confederacion de las Naciones Indigenas de la Amazonia Ecuatoriana (CONFENIAE)
32. Confederacion de Nacionalidades Indigenas de Ecuador (CONAIE)
33. Federation of Native Communities of the Madre de Dios (FENAMAD)
34. Asociacion Interetnica para el Desarollo de la Selva Peruana (AIDESEP)
35. Confederacion de Nacionalides Indigenas del Peru (CONAP)

councils to fully-fledged governments such
as that of the Karen of Myanmar (Burma)
with its own education, tax systems, and
army. Since 1975 the World Council of
Indigenous Peoples (WCIP) has tried to

unite indigenous peoples worldwide round
a common programme. It has not achieved
that objective but enjoys the support of
indigenous peoples' organizations in more
than 20 countries.

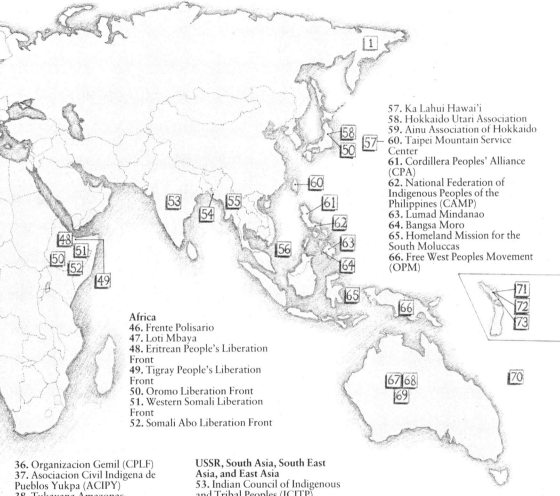

57. Ka Lahui Hawai'i
58. Hokkaido Utari Association
59. Ainu Association of Hokkaido
60. Taipei Mountain Service
Center
61. Cordillera Peoples' Alliance
(CPA)
62. National Federation of
Indigenous Peoples of the
Philippines (CAMP)
63. Lumad Mindanao
64. Bangsa Moro
65. Homeland Mission for the
South Moluccas
66. Free West Peoples Movement
(OPM)

Africa
46. Frente Polisario
47. Loti Mbaya
48. Eritrean People's Liberation
Front
49. Tigray People's Liberation
Front
50. Oromo Liberation Front
51. Western Somali Liberation
Front
52. Somali Abo Liberation Front

36. Organizacion Gemil (CPLF)
37. Asociacion Civil Indigena de
Pueblos Yukpa (ACIPY)
38. Tukayana Amazonas
39. Moshiro
40. Association des Amerindiens
de Guyane francaise (AWARA)
41. Coordinadora de las
Organizaciones Indigenas de la
Cuenca Amazonica(COICA)
42. Uniao dos Nacoes Indigenas
(UNI)
43. AD MAPU
44. Organizacion Regional
Huilliche
45. Asociacion Indigena de la
Republica Argentina (ARIA)

**USSR, South Asia, South East
Asia, and East Asia**
53. Indian Council of Indigenous
and Tribal Peoples (ICITP)
54. Shanti Bahini, Bangladesh
55. National Democratic Front
56. Bakun Residents' Action
Committee

67. National Federation of Land
Councils
68. National Aboriginal and
Islander Legal Services (NAILS)
69. National Coalition of
Aboriginal Organizations
70. Front National pour la
Liberation Kanak Socialiste
(FLNKS)
71. Waitangi Action Committee
72. Maori Unity Movement
73. Maori Peoples Liberation
Movement of Aotearoa

Index of peoples

There are some 5000 distinct indigenous peoples in the world – groups that can be distinguished by linguistic and cultural differences, and geographical separation. This list attempts to provide a picture of the major problems and conflicts confronting indigenous peoples around the world. Many major peoples have been omitted due to lack of space; others, such as the Kurds and Palestinians, because their situations are unrepresentative. Generic names, for example, Aborigines and Inuit, are used, even though the peoples may be made up of many different subgroups. This is a convenience accepted by the peoples themselves. Some names have no definitive spellings – the Santal in India are also spelt Santhal, the Saami are sometimes known as Sami. The preference of the peoples has been used where possible. Population figures are based on often unreliable government statistics and on indigenous information, and in most cases are estimates. Finally, the codes describing the prevailing way of life and major problems can only provide a small clue to the complexity and variation within the lives of indigenous peoples.

Symbols: Prevailing way of life
(H) - hunters, gatherers, trappers, fishers
(P) - pastoralists
(S) - shifting cultivators
(F) - peasant farmers
(U) - large numbers urbanized, assimilated into wider economy, or dependent on welfare from state.

Symbols: Sources of conflict
C - cultural breakdown, tourism, racism, drug-related problems, missionaries
D - dams
E - environmental degradation, pollution
F - deforestation
I - invasions of indigenous lands, colonization
M - mining projects
W - weapons testing, militarization, serious human rights violations

---

ARCTIC AND EUROPE

Inuit and Saami peoples have been relatively protected from colonization because of the harsh climate. In the past, fur traders were attracted to the far north of Canada and Alaska, loggers and miners to the Saami lands in Scandinavia. Today, the regions have oil and mining companies as well as military bases to defend what is seen as the USA's vulnerable northern flank.

Aleut (*Alaska, USA*)
Inuit *100,000 (Alaska, USA 30,000; Canada 25,000; Greenland 42,000; USSR 2000)* (H) (U)
Fewer than 10 per cent dependent on hunting, fishing and trapping but traditional life still important. Inuit Circumpolar Conference, including representation from USSR, aims to bring Inuit together around common programme. **E, M, W**

Saami *60,000 (Finland 4000; Norway 17,000; Sweden 17,000; USSR 2000) 0.1% of population* (P) (U)
Fewer than 10% dependent on reindeer hunting. Nordic Saami Council represented by Saami from Scandinavian countries. **D, E**

CANADA AND NORTH AMERICA

The conditions of most indigenous peoples in Canada and the USA are comparable to those of the poor of the developing countries. Several hundred years of oppression and assimilation have decimated and displaced Indian nations. Today's indigenous peoples are demanding respect for their treaties and control over the resources on their lands.

Canada *(4% of pop.)*
There are 326,000 registered Indians organized in 577 bands, 25,000 Inuit and at least 100,000 – and perhaps as many as 850,000 – Metis and Non-Status Indians. Major peoples include Bella Coola, Blackfoot, Cayugu, Chipewyan, Cree, including James Bay Cree, Dene, Haida, Innu, Inuit, Iroquois, Kwakiutl, Meti, Micmac, Mohawk, Nootka, Oneida, Onondaga, Seneca, Tlingit, Tsimshian, Tuscarova.
Cree 70,000 (H) C D E F M
Dene (H) E F M

Innu (H) W
Mohawk (U) C E
Haida (H) E
Iroquois (U) C

USA *1.5 million including Aleut, Native Alaskans and Inuit in Alaska (0.5% of pop.)*
The Bureau of Indian Affairs recognizes 266 tribes and a further 216 Inuit and Indian communities in Alaska. Major peoples include Apache, Arapaho, Cherokee, Cheyenne, Choctaw, Comanche, Crow, Hopi, Iroquois, Lakota, Navajo, Nez Perce, Pawnee, Pueblo, Shawnee, Shoshone, Oglala Sioux, Uti, Wintu.
Hopi **M**
Iroquois 50,000 (U) C E
Lakota 75,000 (U) C E
Navajo 160,000 (F) **M**
Shoshone (U) **W**

CENTRAL AMERICA

The indigenous peoples of this region – often known as the US backyard – have suffered decades of dictatorships, repression and injustice. Deprived of their lands first by the Spanish colonizers, then by the new landowning elites, many indigenous peoples have been turned into landless peasants. However, traditions remain strong, particularly among the Mayan people who are increasingly organizing to defend their rights.

Total indigenous population 13 million. (F) (S)
Belize *15,000 (10% of pop.) Mayan descent.* (F) (S) **I**

Costa Rica *20,000 (1% of pop.)*
Boruca 1000 **D, I**
Bribri 3500 **I**
Guatuso **I**

El Salvador *960,000 (21% of pop.)*
All indigenous peoples affected by civil war
Lenca (F) **I**
Pipile (F)

Guatemala *3.6 million (50% of pop.)*
Mainly Mayan descent facing intensive government repression for many years.
Chol (S) (F) **W I**
Chuj 26,000 (S) (F) **W I**
Kekchi 340,000 (S) (F) **W I**
Quiche 750,000 (S) (F) **W I**

Honduras *250,000 (7% of pop.)*
Chorti 2000 (S) **I**
Lenca 50,000 (F) **I**
Miskito 45,000

Mexico *8 million (11% of pop.)*
including Aztec descendants facing racism, exclusion from national life, loss of land, and tourism. Refugees from Guatemala along southern border.
Mixe (S) (F) **I C**
Tarahumara (S) (F) **I C**
Yaqui (S) (F) **I C**
Lacandon (S) (F) **I C**
Yucatec (S) (F) **I C**
Huichol (S) (F) **I C**
Nahua (S) (F) **I C**
Zapotec (S) (F) **I C**

Nicaragua *80,000 (3% of population)*
Indigenous peoples forcibly removed from their villages in 1980's and affected by incursions by Contras. Now negotiating regional autonomy.
Miskito 75,000 **W**
Rama 600 (S)
Sumu 5000

Panama *150,000 (6% of pop.)*
Choco and Embera 10,000 (H) **F I**
Guaymi 80,000 (S) **M**
Kuna 50,000 (H) **C F**

SOUTH AMERICA

The total indigenous population is well over 15 million. The majority are highland peoples such as the Quechua and Aymara whose populations exceed 11 million. About 1 million are forest-dwelling peoples who live in the Amazon region. (F)(S)(H)

Argentina *at least 500,000 (0.1% of pop.)*
16 main groups. The majority live along Bolivian and Paraguayan border. Little legal protection and small land base.
Guarani (F) **M I**
Kolla (F) **I**
Mapuche (F) **I**
Mataco (F) **I**
Toba (F) **I**

Bolivia *4 million in highlands and 150,000 in 30 groups in lowlands (66% of pop.)*
Ruthless exploitation of indigenous labour, landlessness, affected by government programme to suppress cocaine production.
Aymara 1 mil **C, I**
Ayoreo **C, I**
Chiquitano **C, I**
Chiriguano **C, I**
Garavo **C, I**
Mojo **C, I**
Quechua 3 mil **C, I**

Brazil *200,000 in 120 nations (1% of pop.)*
among the least assimilated indigenous peoples in the world. The entire region is affected by deforestation, colonization, mining, dam building and land conflicts.
Arara (S)(H) **I**
Arawete (S)(H) **D**
Asurini (S)(H) **D**
Gaviao (S)(H) **D**
Kayapo (S)(H) **D E F**
Kreen-Akrore (S)(H) **I**
Makuxi (S)(H) **I**
Nambikwara (S)(H) **I**
Parakana (S)(H) **D**
Pataxo-Ha-Ha-Hae (S)(H) **I**
Tukano (S)(H) **I M**
Txukurramae (S)(H) **I**
Waimiri-Atraori (S)(H) **I**
Xavante (S) **H I**
Yanomami (S)(H) **E M W**

Chile *1 million (9% of pop.)*
mainly Mapuche in south and small numbers of Aymara in north. Indigenous leaders tortured and killed during Pinochet dictatorship.
Aymara 15,000 (F)
Mapuche 1 mil (F) **D I**

Colombia *300,000 (1% of pop.)*
60 indigenous groups. Some peoples caught up in coca production for drugs traffickers.
Embera (F)(S) **M I**
Guahibo (F)(S) **I**
Guambiano 200,000 (F)(S) **I**
Paez (F)(S)
Tukano (Ufaina) (H) **D**
Wayuu (Guajiro) (F)(S) **M**

Ecuador *3 million in highlands, 70,000 in lowlands (21% of pop.)*
As in Peru and Brazil, the government has earmarked the Amazon region for development, causing conflicts over land.
Colorados Pinchada (H)(S)
Otavala (F) **I**
Quichua 30,000 (F) **I**
Cofan
Secoya 15,000, incl. Siona and Waorani **I M**
Siona (see Secoya) **I M**
Waorani (see Secoya) **E, I, M**
Shuar 20,000 **F M**

French Guiana *4000 (4% of pop.)*
including Arawak.
Guyana *30,000 (3% of pop.)*
Akawaio **D**

Paraguay *100,000 (3% of pop.)*
Indigenous peoples affected by missionaries and colonization projects.
Ache **C F I**
Ayoreo **C F I**
Guarani
Toba-Maskoy

Peru *8 million in highlands, 600,000 in Amazon region (40% of pop.)*
Highland peoples affected by landlessness, lowland peoples face government-sponsored colonization. Human rights abuses by government and Sendero Luminoso guerrillas against indigenous peoples.
Aguaruna Ⓢ Ⓗ I
Amarakaeri Ⓢ Ⓗ I M
Ashaninka Ⓢ Ⓗ D
Aymara Ⓕ C
Matsigenka Ⓢ I
Quechua Ⓕ C
Yagua Ⓢ C

Yanesha (Amuesha) Ⓢ I

Surinam *18,000 (1% of pop.)*
Indigenous peoples affected by civil war.
Lakono Ⓢ M
Karinja Ⓢ M

Venezuela *150,000 (1% of pop.)*
Deforestation, oil exploration and ranching affect indigenous peoples.
Bari Ⓢ Ⓗ C
Panare Ⓢ Ⓗ M I
Piaroa Ⓢ Ⓗ I
Wayuu (Guajiro) Ⓢ Ⓗ
Yanomami (Sanema) Ⓢ Ⓗ E

AFRICA

The way of life and culture of numerous peoples in Africa are affected by civil war, nation-building by centralized states and inappropriate economic projects. Particularly threatened are some 25 million nomadic pastoralists of the Sahel and East Africa and the remaining hunter-gatherers of the Kalahari Desert and the forests of Central Africa.

Afar *110,000 (Ethiopia, Djibouti)* Ⓟ W
Dinka *500,000 (Sudan)* Ⓟ W
Civil war in south.
Eritrean *(Ethiopia)* W
Fipa *(Tanzania)* Ⓟ E
Fulani *6 mil (Chad, Central African Republic, Cameroun, Guinea, Mali, Niger, Nigeria, Senegal)* Ⓟ C, E
Traditional nomadic life restricted.
Hadzabe *1000 (Tanzania)* Ⓗ E F
Hunter-gatherer life restricted due to loss of lands.
Maasai *200,000 (Kenya, Tanzania)* Ⓟ I
Loss of land to wildlife parks.

Nuer *300,000 (Sudan)* Ⓟ W
Civil war in south.
Oromo *(Ethiopia, Kenya)* Ⓕ Ⓟ W
Pygmies *150,000 (Cameroun, Gabon, Zaire)* Ⓗ C F I
Peoples call themselves Efe, Mbuti, Twa etc.
San *62,000 (Angola, Botswana, Namibia)* Ⓗ Ⓕ I W
derogatorily referred to as Bushmen, call themselves Zhu twasi (real people). 60,000 face loss of land to cattle ranchers in Botswana; recruited by South African armed forces in Namibia.
Shilluk
Somali *2 mil outside Somalia (Ethiopia, Somalia, Kenya, Djibouti)* Ⓟ W
Tigrayan *(Ethiopia)* W
Tuareg *900,000 (Algeria, Libya, Niger, Burkina Faso, Mali)* mainly nomadic pastoralists affected by government sedentarization programmes, drought and border bureaucracy.

SOUTH ASIA

Although there was no significant European settlement in Asia, there have been mass migrations of peoples throughout the region. Governments do not wish to recognize that they have indigenous peoples living in isolated areas enjoying considerable independence. In the colonial and post-colonial periods, their territories have been invaded and resources exploited. The peoples referred to in this index have retained distinct cultures and some land base.

Afghanistan *200,000 nomadic and semi-nomadic peoples seriously affected by 10 years of civil war.*
Baluch
Pathan

Bangladesh *600,000 (1% of pop.)*
living in the forested Chittagong Hill Tracts.
Chakma **C D F W**
Khumi
Khyang
Lushai
Marma
Murung
Tripura

India *70 million (7% of pop.)* Ⓕ Ⓢ Ⓗ
Numbers refer to officially recognised indigenous peoples in more than 200 groups, or scheduled tribes. They are widely dispersed and live in the forests and mountains, particularly in the central belt and northeast. Main peoples include Andamese, Bhil, Bhilala, Chencha, Dandami, Garo, Gond, Ho, Khasi, Khond, Kolha, Korku, Malaipantaram, Manipuri, Mizo, Munda, Naga, Oraon, Santal, Ratra, Tadari, Vasara.
Bhil **D F**
Dandami **F**
Gond **D F**
Maipuri **W**
Munda **C F M**
Naga **W**
Santal **F I M**

Iran
Baluch 5 million
Pathan 20 million *(Afghanistan, Iran and Pakistan)*

Pakistan *7.5 million*
2.5 million federally-administered and over 5 million provisionally-administered tribal peoples. Some peoples fiercely defend their local autonomy.
Baluch
Pathan

Sri Lanka *2000*
Vedda 2000
the original inhabitants, living in the eastern forests. Traditional life threatened by dams and colonization.

OCEANIA

Australia: *250,000 Aborigines (2% of pop.)*. Ⓤ **C M**
Main peoples include Gurindji, Kokotha, Manjiljarra, Pitjantatjara, Yirrkala, Yungngora. Aborigines in towns face racism and unemployment; in the country many have no land although some land has been restored to the original owners.

Aotearoa (New Zealand) *300,000 Maoris (10% of pop.) in 11 main groups.* Ⓤ **I C**
Only now is land being restored to some Maoris, but many living in towns are among worst off in society.

Pacific Islands Ⓗ Ⓢ Ⓤ
Region affected by nuclear weapons tests, and economic exploitation by outsiders. Peoples, such as Kanaky, Tahitians, Chamorros on Guam, seeking political independence.
Melanesia
West Papua (1 mil)
Papua New Guinea (3 mil including Dani, Kyaka, Huli, Melpa, Mae Enga, Tsembaga
Fiji 640,000 (44% of pop.)
Kanaky (New Caledonia) 140,000 (45% of pop.)
Solomon Islands 240,000
Vanuatu 140,000
Micronesia
Trust territories 140,000 including the Marshall Islands and Belau
Guam 100,000 (50% of pop.)
Kiribati 56,000
Tuvalu 7500
Caroline Islands
Polynesia
French Polynesia 114,000 (70% of pop.)
W. Samoa 32,000
E. Samoa 158,000
Tonga 98,000
Wallis and Futuna 8,500

EAST ASIA AND USSR

Cambodia, Laos, Vietnam *1 million*
living in the forested mountains affected by wars and recruited by both sides.
Montagnards
Meo
Javai

China *86 million national minorities (7% of pop.), in 55 groups.*
Hui 7.6 mil
Manchu 9 mil
Miao 7.6 mil
Mongolian 5.2 mil
Tibetan 4.7 mil Ⓟ Ⓕ **D I M W**
Uygur 6.6 mil Ⓟ Ⓕ **I W**
Yi 6.6 mil
Zhuang 16 mil

Indonesia *1.5 million (1% of pop.)* Ⓢ Ⓗ
300 ethnic groups speaking 240 languages. When the Dutch withdrew from their colonies, the new government in Jakarta determined to incorporate all the outer islands into the new state. Indigenous peoples have lost land and resources to settlers from Java.
East Timor **W**
Irian Jaya
Kalimantan **D E I**
West Papua 1 mil including Asmat, Amungme, Chimbo, Dani, Dayak, Kapaku, Mae-Enga. **C, D, E, F, I, M, W**

Japan *50,000*
Ainu 50,000 Ⓤ **C**
original inhabitants of island of Hokkaido, affected by racism and tourist exploitation.

Malaysia *71,000 on Peninsula (4% of pop.) in 3 main groups; 500,000 on Eastern Malaysia (50% of pop.).* Ⓢ Ⓗ
Major peoples include Negritos and Sengoi (Peninsula), and Dayak, Iban, Kayan, Kelabit, Kenyah and Penan. Peoples in Eastern Malaysia affected by commercial logging.
Penan 10,000 Ⓗ Ⓕ

Mongolia *1.6 million* Ⓟ
Nomadic and semi-nomadic pastoral activities still remain central to the way of life of Mongolia's 1.6 million people.

Myanmar (Burma) *10 million (30% of pop.)*
living in the forested mountains mountains along the borders including Arakanese, Chin, Kachin, Karen, Palaung, Shan. For nearly 40 years the government has been fighting the indigenous peoples who want regional autonomy.
Karen Ⓢ **W**

Philippines *6.5 million (16% of pop.) belonging to over 50 groups.* Ⓢ Ⓕ
They live in the Cordillera region of Luzon and the forests of Mindanao; a large population of Muslim tribespeople live in the south. Indigenous areas exploited for their resources.
Bangsa Moro **W**
Bontoc **D, F, M**
Hanunoo Ibaloy **D, F, M**
Ifugao **D, F, M**
Isneg
Kalinga **D, F, M**
Kankanai

Taiwan *300,000 in 10 main groups*
Peoples relegated to poverty in the mountains and deprivation and exploitation in the cities.

Thailand *500,000 (1% of pop.) Hill tribes in 9 main groups.*
Most face problems of landlessness as poor farmers from other parts of the country move on to their traditional territory. Commercial logging and opium poppy cultivation also affect some peoples.
Akha
Hmong **C**
Karen **F I**
Lahu
Lisu

USSR *1.4 million (0.5% of pop.)* Ⓟ Ⓤ
Known as "small nationalities" or "small peoples" in 3 main regions: the North and Siberia, the Caucasus, and Central Asia. Like China and the USA, the USSR expanded and incorporates many peoples. Few now practise their traditional herding and hunting way of life; Turkic and Kazakh pastoralists in the south have been largely settled on state farms and co-operatives. Peoples include Chukchi, Karachaevsky, Khakasy, Khanty, Kazakh, Laktsy, Saami, Talysky, Yuit

Resources

World Council of Indigenous Peoples
(International Secretariat)
555 King Edward Avenue
Ottawa, Ontario
Canada K1N 6NS

Central/South America

Alianza Nacional de Profesionales
Indigenas Bilengues AC
Madero 67-60 piso
Despacho 611
Mexico I.D.G.
CP 06000

Uniao dos Nacoes Indigenas (UNI)
C.P.70880
70.000 Brasilia DF
Brazil

ADMAPU
Casilla 1676
Temuco
Chile

Consejo Regional Indigena del Cauca
(CRIC)
Apartado Aereo 516
Popayan
Colombia

Confederacion de Nacionalidades
Indigenas de la Amazonia
Ecuatoriana (CONFENAIE)
Apartado Postal 4180
Quito
Ecuador

Asociacion Interetnica para el
Desarrollo de la Selva Peruana
(AIDESEP)
Av San Eugenio 981
Sta. Catalina
Lima 13
Peru

North America

Indigenous Survival International
Dene National Office
PO Box 2338
Yellowknife N.W.T.
Canada X1A 2P7

Innu Kanatuapatshet
Sheshatshit
Labrador (Ntesinan)
Canada AOP IMO

Metis National Council
116 Middleton Crescent
Saskatoon
Saskatchewan
Canada S75 2W4

Native Council of Canada
72 Metcalf St
Suite 200
Ottawa
Ontario
Canada N6A 3N1

National Indian Brotherhood
Assembly of First Nations
Territory of Akwesasne
Hamilton's Island
Summerstown
Ontario
Canada KOC 2EO

Union of New Brunswick Indians
35 Dedham St
Fredercton
New Brunswick
Canada E3A 2U2

Indian Law Resource Center
601 E Street, SE
Washington DC 20003
USA

International Indian Treaty Council
1259 Folsom
San Francisco
CA 94103
USA

Mohawk Nation/Akwesasne Notes
via Rooseveltown
NY 13683
USA

National Indian Youth Council
201 Hermosa Drive NE
Albuquerque NM87108
USA

Indigenous Women's Network
Centre for Social Change
13621 FM 2769
Austin, TX 78726
USA

Asia
Burma
Human Rights Committee for Non-
Burman Nationalities
PO Box 118
Chiang Mai 50000
Thailand

India
Centre for Tribal Conscientisation
4 Shantadurga
41/5 Karve Rd
Pune 411 038, Maharashtra
India

Indian Council of Indigenous and
Tribal Peoples
28 Mahadev Road
New Delhi
110001
India

Indonesia
OPM (Free Papua Movement)
PO Box 11582
The Hague
Netherlands

Republic of South Moluccas
PO Box 9841
1006 Amsterdam
Netherlands

Japan
Ainu Kyokai
Asahikawa
Sapporo
Hokkaido
Japan

Philippines
Cordillera Peoples' Alliance
Lockbox 596
Garcom Box 7691
DAPO 1300 Domestic Road,
Pasay City
Philipines

Mindanao Tribal Resource Center
PO Box 98
Butuan City 8001
Philippines

Australasia
National Federation of Land Councils
PO Box 3620
Alice Springs
N.T. 5750
Australia

National Organization of Aboriginal
and Islander Legal Services
PO Box 143
Chippendale 2008
N.S.W. Australia

Waitangi Action Committee
PO Box 61140
Otara
Aotearoa
(New Zealand)

Europe
Inuit Circumpolar Conference
PO Box 204 DK 3900
Nuuk
Greenland

Nordic Saami Council
99980 Utsjoki
Finland

NON-GOVERNMENTAL
ORGANIZATIONS
Europe
Anti-Slavery Society
180 Brixton Road
London SW9 6AT
UK

Committee for Indigenous Minority
Research (CIMRA)
5 Caledonian Road
London N1
UK

Forest Peoples Fund
Gaia Foundation
18 Well Walk
London NW3 1LD

Friends of the Earth
(Campaign to save the Rainforests)
26-28 Underwood Street
London N17JQ

Gesellschaft fur Bedrohte Volker
Postfach 2024
D-3400 Gottingen
West Germany

Incomindios,
Schutzenmattstrasse 37
Basel
4051 Switzerland

International Work Group for
   Indigenous Affairs (IWGIA)
Fiolstraede 10
DK-1171 Copenhagen K
Denmark

Minority Rights Group
379/381 Brixton Road
London SW9 7DE

Onaway Trust
275 Main Street
Shadwell
Leeds LS17 8LH
UK

Save the Forests, Save the Planet
International Secretariat
Ecoropa
42 Rue Sorbier
75020 Paris

Survival International
310 Edgware Road
London W2 1DY
UK

Workgroup for Indigenous Peoples
   (WIP)
PO Box 4098
1009 AB Amsterdam
Netherlands

South America

Centro Ecumenico de Documentacao
   e Informacao (CEDI)
Av. Higienpolis 983
CEP 01238, mSao Paulo
Brazil

Comissao Pela Criacao do Parqui
   Yanomami (CCPY)
Rua Manoel da Nobrega 111
3o Andar Conjunto 32
04001 Sao Paulo-SP
Brazil

USA

Cultural Survival
11 Divinity Avenue
Cambridge
MA 02138
USA

Asia

Sahabat alam Malaysia
(Friends of the Earth)
37 Lorong Birch
10250 Penang
Malaysia

RECOMMENDED READING

There is a growing literature on indigenous peoples. Most interesting but often difficult to obtain are the newpapers and journals of indigenous organizations. Several non-indigenous groups also produce regular newletters, books, and increasingly, video films and educational material. For addresses of some of these organizations, see Resources, left. The following short list of books is only meant as a starting point for readers who wish to know more about indigenous peoples.

Anderson R S & Huber, W *The Hour of the Fox: tropical forests, the World Bank and indigenous people in Central India,* University of Washington Press 1988

Beauclerk, John & Narby, Jeremy & Townsend, Janet *Indigenous Peoples: a fieldguide for development,* Oxfam 1988

Brody, Hugh *Living Arctic: hunters of the Canadian north,* Faber & Faber 1987

Brosted J et al *Native Power: the quest for autonomy and nationhood of indigenous peoples,* Universitets forlaget, Bergen 1985

Brown, Dee *Bury my Heart at Wounded Knee,* Picador 1975

Burger, Julian *Report from the Frontier: the state of the world's indigenous peoples,* Zed Press 1987

Clay, Jason *Indigenous peoples and Tropical Forests: models of land use and management from Latin America,* Cultural Survival, Mass. 1988

Colchester, Marcus *Pirates, Squatters and Poachers: the political ecology of dispossession of the native peoples of Sarawak,* Survival International & INSAM, Malaysia 1989

Connolly, Bob & Anderson, R *First Contact: New Guinea's highlanders encounter the outside world,* Penguin 1987

Davis, Shelton *Victims of the Miracle: development and the Indians of Brazil,* Cambridge University Press 1977

Gray, Andrew *The Amerindians of South America,* Minority Rights Group 1987

Hall, Sam *The Fourth World: the heritage of the Arctic and its destruction,* Vintage Books 1988

International Labour Organization *Covenants 107 & 169* concerning indigenous peoples

IWGIA *Self-determination and indigenous peoples:* Sami rights and northern perspectives, Copenhagen 1987

Lewis, I M (ed) *Nationalism and self-determination in the Horn of Africa,* Ithaca Press 1983

Macdonald, Robert *The Maori of Aotearoa – New Zealand,* Minority Rights Group 1989

McKinnan, John & Wanat Bhruksasri (eds) *Highlanders of Thailand,* OUP 1986

Miller, J R *Skyscrapers Hide the Heavens: a history of Indian-white relations in Canada,* University of Toronto Press 1989

Moody, Roger (ed) *The Indigenous Voice Vols 1 & 2,* Zed Press 1988

Rowley, C D *Recovery: the politics of Aboriginal reform,* Penguin 1988

TAPOL *West Papua: the obliteration of a people,* London 1983

von furer-Haimendorf, Christoph *Tribes of India: the struggle for survival,* OUP 1985

INDEX

Photographic credits

Picture sources are listed from left to right and from top to bottom of the page.

Cover Glenna Matoush, Wachiya Collection **2-3** Francesca Pelizzoli **6-7** Bill Leimbach, South American Pictures **8-9** Luke Holland **10** Julian Burger **11** Luke Holland **12** Nigel Smith, The Hutchison Library **13** David Beatty **14-15** S. L. Davis, Dept of Aboriginal Affairs, Australia **16-17** Penny Tweedie, Impact Photos **21** Native American Painting Reference Library; Greg Stevens/Turtle Quarterly **22-3** Native American Painting Reference Library; The Cleveland Press Collection, Cleveland State University Archives **24-5** Simon Trevor, Bruce Coleman; David Coulson **26-7** V. Ziegler; Marcus Colchester **28-9** Canadian High Commission **30-1** Bruce Coleman **32-3** Reproduced by courtesy of the Trustees of the British Museum; Susan Cunningham **35** Brian Moser and Donald Tayler, The Hutchison Library **36-7** South American Pictures **38-9** Mike Wells, Christian Aid; Nancy Durrell Mackenna, The Hutchison Library **40-1** Nicholas Devore, Bruce Coleman **43** Werner Forman Archive **44-5** Sara Mathews; C.B. Frith, Bruce Coleman **46-7** Espen Waehle; Jose Azel, Colorific! **48-9** Francesca Pelizzoli **50-1** Tony Morrison, South American Pictures **52** Fred Ward, Colorific! **53** Tony Morrison, South American Pictures **54-5** Francesca Pelizzoli **56-7** Nick Wood **58-9** The Philbrook Museum of Art, Tulsa, Oklahoma; Fort Sill Museum, Oklahoma **60** Teharentorens **61** Axel Poignant Archive **62-3** Axel Poignant Archive; The Hutchison Library **64-5** Luke Holland; Staatliches Museum Fur Volkerkunde, Munich; Werner Forman **67** Tony Morrison, South American Pictures **68-9** Kurt-Michael Westermann, Syndication **70-1** Maxie Tjampitjinpa, Papunya Tula Artists' Co-operative, Alice Springs **72-3** Brian Moser, Granada Television, The Hutchison Library; Moser/Tayler Collection, The Hutchison Library **74-5** John Hillelson Agency; Bruno Barbey, Magnum Photos **77** Mary Evans Picture Library **78-9** Woodrow Crumbo, The Philbrook Museum of Art, Tulsa, Oklahoma **81** Richard Glazer Danay, Seneca Iroquois National Museum, Salamanca, New York **82-3** Robert

Harding Picture Library; Jerome Tiger, Native American Painting Reference Library **84-5** Batuan Budi, Collection of Dr A.A.M. Djelantik **86-7** Adrian Arbib **88-9** Alain Compost, Bruce Coleman **91** Science Photo Library **93** Stephen Corry, Survival International **94-5** Survival International; CAP, Third World Network **97-9** David Beatty **100-1** Ester Hernandez **102-3** Magnum Photos **105** Betty Whyoulter, Australia **106-7** Susan Cunningham **108-9** Robert Harding Picture Library **111** Amders H. Anderson, Tibet Photo Archive **112-13** Bryan and Cherry Alexander Photography **114-15** Pereira, Greenpeace **116-17** Amnesty International **118-19** The Hutchison Library **120-1** Robert Harding; J. Hartley/Oxfam; Panos Pictures; Steve McCurry, Magnum Photos **123** Richard Green, Turtle Quarterly **125** A. Greensmith, Ardea London Ltd **126-7** Survival International; Penny Tweedie, Impact **128-9** Novosti **130-1** Michael Stuckey, Susan Griggs Agency **132-3** Luke Holland **134-5** Conselho Nacional dos Seringueiros Uniao das nacoes indigenas-uni **137** Mary Evans **139** Associated Press **141** Ron Anderson, copyright 1987, The Oklahoma Publishing Company **142-3** New Breed, Saskatchewan **144-5** Irven DeVore, Anthro-Photo File Cambridge MA **146-7** Department of Indian Affairs and Northern Development **148-9** Piers Cavendish, Reflex Picture Agency **150-1** Piers Cavendish, Reflex Picture Agency **152-3** Andy Fernando and Brenda Snyder; Northwest Indian Fisheries Commission, USA **154-5** Penny Tweedie, Impact; Aboriginal Medical Service Co-operative **157** Jorgren Brochner Jorgensen, IWGIA **158-9** Orlando Brito-Brasilio, Cultural Survival; UN photo **160-1** Sheila Aikman; Ana-Cecilia Gonzales, Reflex Picture Agency **162-3** Courtesy of Survival International, IWGIA, Amnesty International, The Anti-Slavery Society **164-5** Susan Cunningham **166-7** Melvyn C. Goldstein and Cynthia Beall **168-9** Carl Purcell, Colorific!; Gil Hanley **170-1** Tony Morrison, South American Pictures **172-3** Piers Cavendish, Reflex Picture Agency; Marsha A. Gomez, Center for Social Change, USA **174-5** Bryan and Cherry Alexander Photography **176-7** NASA, Science Photo Library

ACKNOWLEDGMENTS

Gaia Books would like to extend warm thanks to everyone involved in the making of this book. First to Julian Burger for his generosity, co-operation and unfailing enthusiasm; to the many indigenous people who offered invaluable knowledge and support; to all who contributed text, pictures and reference; to those who devoted time to reading the text and giving helpful comments, particularly Joji Carino, Jason Clay, Marcus Colchester, Andrew Gray, Roger Moody, Norman Myers, Geoff Nettleton, Sharon Venne; to Ann Savage for her beautiful illustrations, patience and expertise; the Indigenous Women's Network and the many organizations and agencies who helped with information and images. The team would also particularly like to thank Joss Pearson for sharing her knowledge and giving support; Penny Cowdry for consistent and good-humoured administrative help; Lynette Beckford for co-ordination and support; also, Imogen Bright, Jonathan Hilton, Odile Louis-Sydney, On Yer Bike, Ken and Barry at Marlin Graphics, and Martin and Robert at Technographics; also Mike Pilley at Radius.

Note
The data for this book has been gathered from many different sources and represent as far as possible the views of indigenous peoples. Every effort has been made to present the most reliable and up-to-date view of rapidly changing situations. Do write to us at Gaia Books and tell us your reactions. We would welcome any feedback and suggestions to include in the forthcoming FUTURES titles.

Other Gaia books published by Doubleday:

The Gaia Atlas of Planet Management
by Dr. Norman Myers
0-385-19072-7

State of the Ark
by Lee Durrell
0-385-23668-9